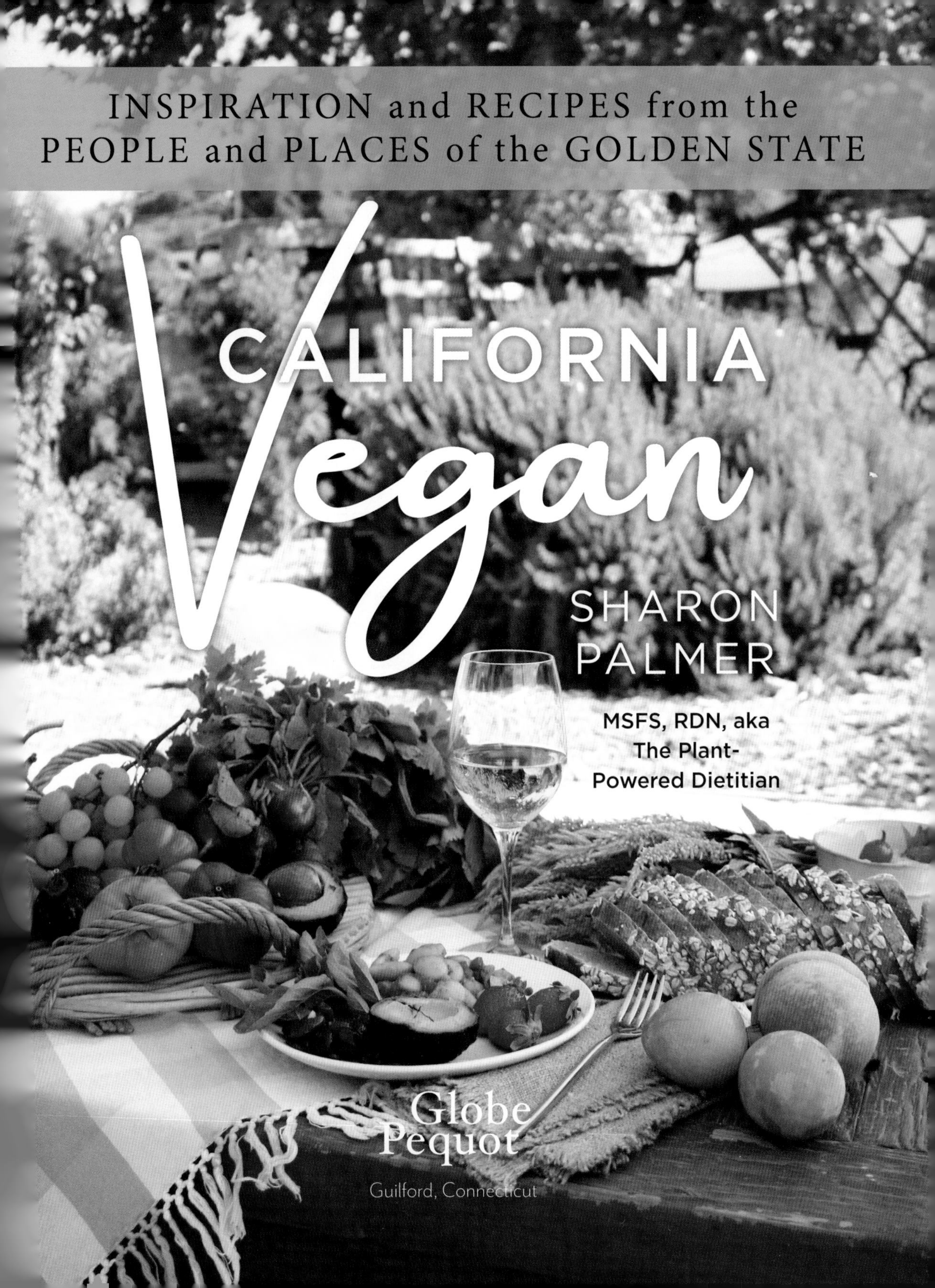

INSPIRATION and RECIPES from the
PEOPLE and PLACES of the GOLDEN STATE

CALIFORNIA Vegan

SHARON PALMER

MSFS, RDN, aka
The Plant-
Powered Dietitian

Globe
Pequot

Guilford, Connecticut

Globe Pequot

An imprint of The Rowman & Littlefield Publishing Group, Inc.
4501 Forbes Blvd., Ste. 200
Lanham, MD 20706
www.rowman.com

Distributed by NATIONAL BOOK NETWORK

British Library Cataloguing in Publication Information available

Library of Congress Control Number: 2020950428

ISBN 978-1-4930-5050-5 (cloth : alk. paper)
ISBN 978-1-4930-5051-2 (electronic)

∞™ The paper used in this publication meets the minimum requirements of American National Standard for Information Sciences—Permanence of Paper for Printed Library Materials, ANSI/NISO Z39.48-1992

Contents

Foreword

Plant-based eating is *so California*. It's in the very DNA of this perpetually optimistic, sun-drenched state to care about the health of all people, as well as the health of the planet and animals. As a writer, director, and producer of films portraying the vegan lifestyle, I've had the opportunity to talk to people all over the state in virtually all walks of life—from those just released from prison to farm workers to working moms to world-famous movie stars. What do all of these people have in common? They all want the best for their children. They want their children to grow up to be strong and healthy, without the gnawing presence of obesity or type 2 diabetes to lessen the quality and length of their lives. They want to leave a planet that will offer clean skies and plenty of water and food. They also want to leave a beautiful planet, with an array of diverse ecosystems and wildlife, such as Monarch butterflies, honeybees, spotted owls, garter snakes, tiger salamanders, and tri-colored blackbirds—all of which are currently threatened in California. And they want to instill compassion for all living things, including farm animals.

It's becoming increasingly clear that our diets are perhaps the greatest chance to making this future and these dreams actualize. It reduces the chance of obesity and chronic disease. It lessens our footprint on the planet by reducing greenhouse gas emissions. It preserves our precious resources, such as water, soil, and air. It nurtures more biodiverse ecosystems. And it saves the lives of millions of animals.

As a local Californian, I'm proud to say that my community is one of the leaders in the plant-based movement. In every corner of the state—in every borough, village, farm community, and urban area—people are shining the light on plants in cool, innovative ways. Whether it's the hip,

edgy food stand serving up vegan tacos in Highland Park, the farm-to-fork capital of Sacramento promoting seasonal vegetable gardens in home backyards, or the Silicon Valley startup creating an amazing plant-based innovation that sweeps the nation—you can find it all here, and then some. There is so much good stuff happening every single day, which truly feeds my soul.

I'm not saying that California holds the patent on plant-based eating; I've observed firsthand vegan communities all across the nation, each making an impressive mark on the movement. What I *am* saying is that California has always stood up as a sort of beacon for a casual, farm-fresh, globally inspired, health-oriented, vegan-friendly way of eating that can infuse your own eating style with good vibrations. Whether you've been vegan for decades or you're completely new to the plant-based movement, one thing's for sure: Sharon's style of California cooking is simple, delicious, and addictive. I know from personal experience working with Sharon that she represents a sort of plant-based cooking and eating style that symbolizes California, capturing the soil, sun, water, and people of this place all in a single breath. So, let Sharon inspire your own vegan eating style no matter where you live. Join her in celebrating the plant-based movement in your own hometown. Let's all join together for the very health of our future.

Kip Andersen
Film Writer, Director, Producer

1

Homegrown

What is a "California vegan"? Is it the middle-aged woman in Berkeley who has been fermenting vegetables, baking sourdough bread, and sprouting mung beans long before it was a thing? Is it the Buddhist living in San Diego who aspires to a lifestyle that does no harm? Is it a 27-year-old Mexican American animal-welfare advocate living in hip Echo Park who just discovered the vegan lifestyle? Is it the 103-year-old cardiothoracic surgeon who attributes his vibrant long life to his plant-based lifestyle? Is it the former cattle farmer in the Central Valley who just couldn't live with the impacts of his agriculture for another day? Is it the young, tattooed San Francisco chef who worships vegetables and rises early to see what awaits him at the farmers market? Is it the African American football player who powers his performance with plants? Yes, these are all California vegans—real people whom I've met and broken bread with. And there are so many more faces and places that represent the rising plant-based movement in this forever sunny, optimistic state.

Veganism is on the rise, with 90% of vegetarians considering making a switch to veganism and 42% of meat eaters planning on eating less meat or cutting it out completely. And while the nation—and even the globe—is getting its plant-based groove on, this diet trend is even hotter

Freshly harvested, petite heirloom carrots at a California farmers market.

in California, the land of the health-minded, eco-conscious, animal-loving, vegetable-growing, and globally aware. I lived in the San Gabriel foothills, within the county of Los Angeles, for most of my life. LA was voted the most vegan-friendly city in the US by both *The Vegan World* and *Plant Based News*, thanks to its large concentration of vegan restaurants. Just look around the state, and it all starts to make sense. It is here that celebrity chefs like Tal Ronen, Roberto Martin, and Matthew Kenney have put vegan dining on the map. It is here that a slew of Hollywood stars talk about their plant-based lifestyle, including Pamela Anderson, Ellen Degeneres, Leonardo DiCaprio, and Joaquin Phoenix. And it is in this state that animal-welfare organizations, such as Mercy for Animals and The Humane Society, are headquartered or maintain active offices.

When I think about eating like a California vegan, I can't help but picture an outdoor wooden table, groaning against its burden of dishes made from freshly harvested produce prepared in a simple, straightforward way, straight from the farms nourished by the California Mediterranean climate. Year-round local produce, such as tomatoes, eggplant, citrus, berries, peaches, olives, pistachios, chickpeas, and brown rice—of course served with a locally produced wine—are the stars of the meal. While this vision may resonate with most, being a California vegan is about so much more than that. It encompasses food cultures from every corner of the globe, including countries in Central America, Africa, Asia, and Europe, which have inspired the trademark fusion of California farms and its easy lifestyle with the beauty of traditional, diverse foodways.

California vegan is also about living a lean, green, vibrant, long life, compliments of the most healthful and eco-friendly diet on the planet. No wonder a long line of plant-forward health thinkers have found their way to the sunny state. The first US vegan society, established in 1960, was founded by Catherine Nimmo, a vegan Dutch doctor who moved to California. The publication of the classic book *Diet for a Small Planet* in 1971 by Berkeley-graduate Frances Moore Lappé introduced the world to a plant-based diet to help preserve the earth. About the same time, California hippies started embracing the plant-based movement in places like The Farm—a commune of San Francisco hippies who turned to soy for protein sources. The health arm of the vegan movement started growing out of California, with the Loma Linda University School of Public Health launching the Adventist Health Studies in 1958, which analyzed the health of Seventh Day Adventists who practiced plant-based lifestyles. And John McDougal's influential plant-based diet program came to St. Helena, California, in 1986.

This is about the same time my own plant-based California epiphany occurred. I had tossed fresh cassettes of *The Beach Boys Surfin' USA* and *The Go-Go's Vacation* in the passenger seat of my baby blue Plymouth Duster to be played on repeat as I headed down the I-5 en route to Southern California. The year was 1981 and, filled with expectation, I was about to make my way to Loma Linda University, a meat-free campus and future Blue Zone (this would come in 2004, when Dan Buettner identified Loma Linda as the location in the US with the largest volume of centenarians), where I was enrolled to finish my nutrition studies and become a registered dietitian. It was a typical overcast morning in Seattle, and a box in the trunk of my car was packed with the nubby sweaters, drab khaki chinos, and sturdy navy corduroys of my Northwestern youth—metaphors for my life there. I just could not comprehend how out of place my wardrobe was about to become. Like my clothing, my entire world—food, culture, customs, attitudes—was about to be rocked, and it would never, ever go back to the way it was before.

On the second day of driving, I spied my very first California sunset—all hot pink, sassy peach, and neon lavender—with the silhouette of palm trees in the forefront. To this day, I smile like a contented cat when I see one of those palm-lined sunsets. I have to admit, it's the same sort of smile that appears on my face today when I stroll into a farmers market on a bright Saturday morning, discover a throng of plant-based food trucks along a gritty downtown LA street, or spend a day in enlightened Ojai among citrus, avocado, and lavender farms. On that warm, late August afternoon so long ago, I parked my car and walked along a California beach town sidewalk to see the sights, stretch my legs, and get a bite to eat at a Mexican restaurant (my first of many such meals to come!). The women were dressed in every color of that California sunset and beyond. Some were nearly professionally glammed up, while others were as fresh-faced as a flower child. The men ranged from beach bum Adonises to everyday dads toting beach bags with their kids. People from every culture and ethnicity seemed to be gathered on that sidewalk that day. They smiled, chirping a friendly greeting to me, a total stranger. It was on that day that I fell in love with California—its people, places, and foodways.

Since then, I've lived in and traveled all over the Golden State, from north to south, east to west, sea to mountain to desert, feeling the essence and optimism of its people, places, and foods. As a plant-based dietitian, I have become intimately familiar with the food traditions of thousands of people in this state over more than three decades. I also have come to appreciate that California is a unique place. In the place I call my bioregion, once dinosaurs, followed by mammoths and sloths, roamed the territory, now taken over by gray foxes, bobcats, and mountain lions. You can thank major tectonic plates and the San Andreas Fault for spurring the geologic diversity behind my back door, granting me glimpses of soaring granite mountains, which wore down to eventually reveal plains and deserts and to nourish fertile valleys. Today, California is the golden land of agriculture, producing over one-third of the country's vegetables and two-thirds of its fruits and nuts. The state is now a leader in the sustainable farming movement, with a flurry of buzz surrounding urban gardens, CSAs, organic farms, farmers markets, and renewable farming systems.

My heart has always been in the soil, an attribute I trace back to my farming parents. During the Great Depression and World War II, a small boy named Glen Palmer grew up on a picturesque farm in Minnesota,

Sharon and her family enjoying a *plein air* plant-based dinner.

where corn was a primary crop and his mother had a robust vegetable garden that supplied the family through the long cold winter. She canned vegetables, dried corn, and made bread from Minnesota wheat. At the same time, a little girl named Cora Pemberton was growing up on a farm in Arkansas, which was a subsistence farm that supplied the family with everything it needed—even in the lean years of the Depression. A bit of sorghum was grown to boil down into a prized sweetener, fields of corn provided grain, and peanuts were harvested and dried in the barn and then roasted in a big iron pot over a fire. A large, diverse garden supplied the family with okra, carrots, onions, tomatoes, potatoes, turnips, squash, and lots of beans—the primary source of protein. Pear, apple, and peach trees furnished fruits, and the forest bestowed wild greens and berries. On most days, pots of beans and greens were simmering on the wood-burning stove, with a pan of crispy cornbread baking in the oven. A plant-based meal made in heaven! In fact, most cultures around the world focused on simple plant foods and eating patterns like these for sustenance, before industrialization made the current high-meat, processed foods diet so ubiquitous. These plant-based diets were considered "the poor man's diet," but now we know that this style of eating was the most healthful, "rich" diet pattern of all.

As teenagers, Glen and Cora both ended up moving to Idaho on farms right next to one another. They eventually eloped and move to Seattle, where I was born—along with my brother and sister. They took on a primarily vegetarian diet for health and moral reasons, and maintained their farming roots in the woodsy, plentiful Northwest, learning about the soils, climate, and native plants; planting a large vegetable garden and fruit trees; putting up rows of pretty jars of peaches and tomatoes in the summer, baking rough grain breads during the week; and practicing a simple, healthful lifestyle. I believe this connection to the soil and healthful plant-based eating is why my parents were still vibrant into their late eighties. Maybe it's why I'm fortunate enough to be the picture of health, too; people often guess me to be at least ten years younger than my true age. Maybe it's also why I obtained my graduate degree in sustainable food systems, and made my dream of living on the land in Ojai, California, come true.

Connections to plants and the earth come from all around us, whether we live in a city dwelling, suburban home, or farmstead. The acorns falling from California's majestic live oaks once were a primary food source for the Native Americans. The age-old forests are filled with nutrient-rich foods, including berries, mushrooms, and nettles. Farmers have brought seeds from all over the world, from Africa, Asia, and Central America, to plant in our soils and give rise to the pungent, hot, sweet, and bitter flavors so characteristic of cooking styles, whether it be from Morocco, Central America, or the Caribbean. California can now lay claim to some of the finest-quality foods, such as wines, olive oils, citrus fruits, nuts, and avocados, in the world! You can walk through a farmers market and enjoy perfectly ripe seasonal produce—soil still clinging to its roots—every day of the year. You name it, it is possible, here.

In this book, I will share stories of people, place, traditions, and cooking in order to inspire your own peaceful, reverent, and celebratory relationship with plant-based food. I hope that you take some lessons from these pages to meld into your own life experience, no matter where you live. Embrace the essence of the California spirit in your own plant-based lifestyle. Take the very best parts of it with you, and fold it into your kitchen, table, and life. I will be there with you every step of the way along your path. Let's take the journey together!

—Sharon

Gluten-Free Note:

Recipes may easily be made gluten-free with the following tips:

* Substitute gluten-free flour blend for wheat-based flour in baked recipes or for breading.
* Choose gluten-free soy sauce.
* Substitute cornstarch for wheat flour when it is used for thickening.
* Use gluten-free breadcrumbs.
* Use gluten-free oats.
* Substitute a gluten-free grain (i.e., quinoa, sorghum, brown rice, millet) for a gluten-containing grain (i.e., farro, couscous, barley, bulgur).
* Use gluten-free bread or buns.
* Use gluten-free pasta or noodles.
* Use gluten-free pastry dough (in Tart).
* Use gluten-free vegetarian chili (in Haystacks)

Blackberry Pecan Cobbler

My mother hand-copied this recipe, which came from my Great Aunt Prussia, on a now-faded, much-used recipe card, turning to it hundreds of times over the years. This was a dessert that was all about making something of nothing: any fruit on hand—berries picked in the forest, peaches put up for the winter, or apples falling from the tree—could be called upon. It features a humble sweet biscuit dough on the bottom, and simmered fruit on the top. I borrowed from my Northwest traditions and included blackberries, which grow like weeds there, and pecans—another nod to my mother's Southern roots.

SERVES 8

For the blackberry filling:

3 cups blackberries (fresh or frozen), unsweetened

¼ cup sorghum syrup (or pure maple syrup)

1 tablespoon lemon juice

1 teaspoon cinnamon

For the dough:

1 cup flour

½ cup organic cane sugar

1 teaspoon baking powder

Pinch salt

2 tablespoons dairy-free margarine

½ cup plant-based milk, plain, unsweetened

For the topping:

¼ cup coarsely chopped pecans

Place blackberries, sorghum syrup (or maple), lemon juice, and cinnamon in a medium pot and bring to a boil. Simmer for about 5 minutes, until berries are juicy.

Preheat oven to 350°F.

Mix together flour, sugar, baking powder, and salt in a small mixing bowl. Cut in margarine with a fork. Stir in plant-based milk just until moistened.

Spray a 9 x 13-inch baking dish with nonstick cooking spray. Drop dough into bottom of baking dish by the spoonful.

Cover with fruit.

Sprinkle with pecans.

Place in the top rack of the oven and bake for about 40 minutes, until dough is tender.

May serve with plant-based ice cream or coconut cream.

Nutrition information per serving: 163 calories, 6 g total fat, 1 g saturated fat, 0 mg cholesterol, 11 mg sodium, 27 g carbohydrates, 4 g fiber, 10 g sugar, 3 g protein

How to make aquafaba

Aquafaba is a bean liquid, which can take the place of eggs when whipped into a thick foam. Just place the drained liquid from one 15-ounce can of beans in a mixing bowl, and beat with an electric mixer until thick and foamy (about 3–4 minutes) or even longer (about 5 minutes) to form stiff peaks. This replaces two eggs in a recipe.

Vegan Johnny Cake with Sausage

My father grew up on a farm in Minnesota, where the family raised corn as one of their main crops. Their sweet corn was dried for cooking all year long, which sustained the family, along with supplies from their kitchen garden and local foods from town, such as good ol' Minnesota wheat. Johnny cake is a traditional American food, which has a history in my father's home place, too. Made of cornmeal and flour, this bread was often cooked in a skillet to crisp, golden perfection. Whatever was available in the kitchen went into the batter to turn it into a meal-in-one. I made this dish into a plant-based version, with the magic of aquafaba, vegan sausage, and whole sweet corn as a nod to my father's Minnesota traditions.

SERVES 12

½ cup aquafaba (see note on opposite page 10)

1 cup whole wheat flour

1 cup all-purpose wheat flour

2 cups yellow cornmeal

½ teaspoon salt (optional)

2 tablespoons baking powder

1½ cups plant-based milk, plain, unsweetened

½ cup vegetable oil

¼ cup pure maple syrup

1 cup frozen sweet corn, thawed, drained

9 ounces vegan sausage, prepared, sliced

Place aquafaba in a mixing bowl and beat over medium speed for about 3–4 minutes, until thick and foamy.

Preheat oven to 400°F.

Place whole wheat and all-purpose wheat flours, cornmeal, salt (optional), and baking powder in a medium mixing bowl.

Make a well in the center of the dry ingredients, and gently pour in whipped aquafaba, plant-based milk, oil, and maple syrup.

Gently fold liquid ingredients into dry ingredients until well combined (do not over-stir).

Fold in corn and vegan sausage.

Spray a large skillet with nonstick cooking spray. Pour batter into the skillet and place on the top rack of the oven.

Bake for about 45 minutes, until tender and golden on top.

Remove and slice into wedges.

Note: May add additional ingredients to batter, as desired, including jalapeño slices, cilantro, roasted sweet pepper slices, chopped onions, and shredded zucchini.

Nutrition information per serving: 354 calories, 14.5 g total fat, 2 g saturated fat, 0 mg cholesterol, 206 mg sodium, 41 g carbohydrates, 5 g fiber, 5 g sugar, 10 g protein

Black-Eyed Peas and Greens

Nothing spells pure comfort food like this satisfying, hearty recipe inspired by my mother's classic Southern style of cooking. My mother's favorite dish is black-eyed peas, which is a good-luck food often served for New Year's. Serve it with the "Cheesy" Baked Grits (page 15) for an entirely satisfying plant-based meal.

SERVES 8

1 pound dried black-eyed peas

1 tablespoon olive oil

1 large onion, diced

3 stalks celery, sliced

3 cloves garlic, minced

1 teaspoon smoked paprika

½ teaspoon cayenne pepper

2 teaspoons oregano

1 teaspoon dry mustard

2 bay leaves

5 cups vegetable broth

1 small bunch (8 ounces) fresh greens (collard, mustard, beet, dandelion, or spinach greens), sliced

Salt (optional)

Soak black-eyed peas in water overnight.

Rinse and drain soaked black-eyed peas.

In a large pot, heat olive oil and add onion, celery, and garlic, sautéing for 9 minutes.

Add smoked paprika, cayenne pepper, oregano, dry mustard, bay leaves, vegetable broth, and black-eyed peas to the pot. Stir well and bring to a simmer.

Reduce heat to medium, cover, and cook for about 50–60 minutes, until tender. May add additional water as needed to replace liquid lost to evaporation. Should make a thick, stew-like consistency.

Add sliced greens and cook for an additional 2 minutes, just until wilted yet bright green. May season with salt, as desired.

Makes about 1 cup per portion.

Nutrition information per serving: 232 calories, 3 g total fat, 0 g saturated fat, 0 mg cholesterol, 673 mg sodium, 40 g carbohydrates, 8 g fiber, 6 g sugar, 14 g protein

"Cheesy" Baked Grits

One of my mother's favorite dishes of all times to prepare was a "cheesy" baked grits, which the family adored. I borrowed from her favorite food traditions to create this Southern cozy food. Combine it with the Black-Eyed Peas and Greens (page 12) and you'll enjoy a plant-powered meal in one, good for the mind, body, and soul.

SERVES 8

For the "cheddar" cashew cheese:

1 cup raw cashews (soaked in water for at least an hour, up to overnight, in refrigerator)

1 clove garlic

½ teaspoon turmeric

¼ teaspoon smoked salt

¼ teaspoon white pepper

3 tablespoons nutritional yeast

2 tablespoons lemon juice

6–7 tablespoons plant-based milk, plain, unsweetened

For the baked "cheesy" grits:

3 cups plant-based milk, plain, unsweetened

2 cups water

2 tablespoons dairy-free margarine

1½ cups uncooked grits

¼ teaspoon salt (optional)

¼ teaspoon white pepper

1 cup "cheddar" cashew cheese

To make the "cheddar" cashew cheese: Rinse and drain water from cashews and place in a blender or food processor, along with garlic, turmeric, smoked salt, white pepper, nutritional yeast, and lemon juice. Add 4 tablespoons of plant-based milk. Blend cashew cheese until it makes a smooth, creamy texture. Add additional plant-based milk, 1 tablespoon at a time, to achieve desired texture. Between processing, stop and scrape down sides, as needed. Makes 1 cup cashew cheese.

To make the baked "cheesy" grits: Place plant-based milk, water, and margarine in a medium pot and bring to a boil. Add uncooked grits with salt (optional) and white pepper. Cover and cook for about 30 minutes, until tender and creamy, stirring frequently.

Preheat oven to 375°F.

Stir 1 cup of "cheddar" cashew cheese into the grits. Place in a large (2-quart) casserole dish. Place in oven on top rack and bake, uncovered, for about 40 minutes, until slightly golden on top.

Makes about ¾ cup of grits per serving.

Nutrition information per serving: 332 calories, 17 g total fat, 3 g saturated fat, 0 mg cholesterol, 144 mg sodium, 35 g carbohydrates, 3 g fiber, 2 g sugar, 12 g protein

Fried Green Tomatoes

Fried green tomatoes originated as a way to make use of every single fruit of the garden—even a hard green tomato, which came too late on the vine and would never mature. Before recent times, Americans always endured times of hunger, and our food cultures and traditions are based upon the idea of making something out of nothing. With a reverent nod to my mother's Southern food traditions, this recipe is inspired by my own garden, which always produces its fair share of large green tomatoes that stubbornly stay firm but are perfect for this most satisfying of dishes. Serve with Vegan Ranch Dressing (page 42) or Almond Rosemary Cream (page 73) for an excellent creamy dipping sauce.

SERVES 4

½ cup all-purpose wheat flour

½ cup cornmeal

½ teaspoon Cajun seasoning blend

¼ teaspoon black pepper

¼ teaspoon salt (optional)

½ cup plant-based milk, plain, unsweetened

½ lemon, juiced

1½ teaspoons chia seeds

4 large, green, immature tomatoes

¼ cup vegetable oil

Prepare batter by mixing together flour, cornmeal, Cajun seasoning blend, black pepper, and salt (optional) in a small bowl, then transfer this breading mixture to a small dish. Mix plant-based milk, lemon juice, and chia seeds in another small bowl and allow to sit for 5 minutes to thicken, then stir well.

Slice tomatoes into thick slices, about ½ inch thick (about five slices per tomato, depending on size).

Heat half of the oil in a large skillet or griddle over medium heat.

Prepare tomatoes by dipping each slice into the plant-based milk mixture, then coating each side of the slice with the flour mixture. Place coated tomato slices in the skillet with hot oil, until it is filled with tomato slices, and cook each slice over medium heat until golden (about 5–6 minutes on each side), then turn each slice to cook the other side until golden. Add the remaining oil as needed to cook all of the tomato slices.

Nutrition information per serving: 309 calories, 15 g total fat, 2 g saturated fat, 186 mg sodium, 0 mg cholesterol, 40 g carbohydrates, 4 g fiber, 8 g sugar, 6 g protein

Chocolate Zucchini Cake with Frosting

This ooey-gooey, fudgy chocolate cake highlights how veggies can add so much moisture to recipes, such as zucchini in a luscious cake. This recipe is handed down from my mother, with a vegan twist thanks to aquafaba. We always had zucchinis coming out of our ears in the summertime; thus, we were always looking for ingenious ways to use up this versatile vegetable.

MAKES 15 SERVINGS

For the cake:

½ cup aquafaba (see note on page 10)

1 cup coconut palm sugar (or brown sugar)

½ cup dairy-free margarine, soft

1 teaspoon vanilla

½ cup plant-based milk, plain, unsweetened

1 teaspoon vinegar

¼ cup cocoa powder

1¾ cup all-purpose flour

½ cup almond, coconut, or pecan meal

1 tablespoon ground flaxseed

1 teaspoon baking powder

1 teaspoon baking soda

1 teaspoon cinnamon

2 cups shredded zucchini

1 cup dairy-free dark chocolate chips

For the frosting (optional):

2 tablespoons dairy-free margarine, soft

1 teaspoon vanilla

2 tablespoons cocoa powder

2 cups powdered sugar

1 tablespoon plant-based milk, plain, unsweetened

Preheat oven to 350°F.

Add aquafaba and coconut palm sugar (or brown sugar) in a large bowl and use an electric mixer to whip until white and stiff (about 3–5 minutes).

Gently stir in margarine, vanilla, plant-based milk, and vinegar.

In a separate bowl, combine cocoa powder, flour, meal, flaxseed, baking powder, baking soda, and cinnamon.

Gradually fold in the dry ingredients into the mixing bowl, gently stirring only to combine ingredients.

Stir in zucchini and chocolate chips gently.

Spray a medium baking dish (11 x 7-inch) with nonstick spray and pour batter into the dish, spreading evenly.

Place in oven and bake for 45–50 minutes, until fork inserted in center comes out clean. Makes a very moist, fudgy cake. Remove from oven and cool.

To make the frosting: Mix margarine, vanilla, cocoa powder, powdered sugar, and plant-based milk with an electric mixer in a small bowl until smooth and fluffy. When cake is cool, frost surface.

Slice into fifteen squares.

Nutrition information per serving: 405 calories, 24 g fat, 270 mg sodium, 52 g carbohydrates, 3 g fiber, 30 g sugar, 4 g protein

2

Plant-Powered Eating *a la* Los Angeles

Pozole, a traditional Latin hominy stew with ancho-chili broth, cashew cream, and avocados served at Gracias Madre. "Devoted," an Indonesian grain bowl with forbidden black rice, roasted beets, squash, edamame, and kale in a peanut sauce dished up at Café Gratitude. Spicy ramen with sunflower seed broth, spicy paste, king oyster mushrooms, bean sprouts, and chili threads at Ramenhood. These are just a few of my favorite plant-based meals in LA eateries. But Los Angeles wasn't always the vegan mecca it is today. The City of Angels took a long, meandering road to become the eclectic hot spot for indulgent veganism you'll find in virtually every borough.

Graffiti art depicting fruits on display in the Arts District of Downtown Los Angeles.

After graduating from the dietetics program at Loma Linda University, I worked as a dietitian in the Inland Empire of Southern California for several years before moving to the big, sprawling metropolis of Los Angeles in 1991, just in time to observe the horrendous Rodney King beating and the resulting LA riots. These were the days of the AIDs crisis, recession, violence, and natural disasters, like earthquakes, fires, and mudslides, which all pounded LA like a sledgehammer. Much of Los Angeles was really rough around the edges, with grimy sidewalks, decaying neighborhoods, and tacky strip malls.

Beneath all of that crime, grime, and sprawl, you could catch a glimpse of some former, gilded time, if you looked closely enough. An Art Deco facade behind a glow-in-the-dark Quinceanera shop in the Garment District. The bones of a prohibition-era bowling alley in the skyline. Weathered redbrick walls covered with Dali-esque graffiti art. And that hint of glamour took on a special patina because it was juxtaposed against urban decay. It was as if Los Angeles had been slumbering since its glittering, golden 1920s, awaiting a kiss from its fans to restore the intricately carved facades and painted ceilings to their former glory, but with a cool, edgy gleam. Indeed, out of this dismal landscape came a powerful cultural force that would creep up on LA and make it the iconic symbol of fierce diversity, tolerance, and artistic expression it is today.

Los Angeles is a city of contrasts. To be sure, not all of the streets were dingy in those days. After all, LA had always drawn the wealthy and "beautiful" to playgrounds like Beverly Hills, Palos Verde, and Malibu, which seemed to power through every recession and setback. And the Arts and Crafts and Mid-Century cottage neighborhoods in Pasadena, the San Fernando Valley, and Los Feliz attracted yuppies like bees to honey. But somehow the rough urban veneer of the city gave even the shinier neighborhoods some sort of street cred. Los Angeles always felt like the center of the universe, where every trend, whim, and fashion seemed to take root first. This was truly the place you could fly your freak flag and be true to yourself without much fear of repercussion. The city had a longstanding commitment to expression, art, music, architecture, and theater. And the people—of every culture, gender, walk of life, and corner of the world—came together into one of the grandest melting pots in the world. These factors surely contributed to the virtual cultural bomb that exploded in Los Angeles at the turn of the twenty-first century.

You can give the food scene a big thank you for the cultural renaissance that occurred in Los Angeles during this time. A force of young, multicultural, inked-up chefs rose up in the city. They could not afford to open eateries in the tony neighborhoods of Beverly Hills or Santa Monica. But what about a small café on a little-known street in downtown, or a dilapidated borough no foodie had ever set foot in? These young chefs, who were raised on James Beard and the Food Network, lived and breathed food. They foraged in the hills for wild herbs, frequented tiny ethnic markets, and rose early to shop at the farmers market, where a year-round cornucopia of plants were harvested just a couple of hours before. These visionaries were in tune with the cultural food traditions of the city, which had never met a global flavor it didn't like. They understood how to meld those flavors—Ethiopian, Lebanese, Vietnamese, Filipino, and beyond—into what had always been California's fresh, casual, cultural aesthetic. Before you knew it, LA was on the food map, and entire communities and food cultures were revitalized as patrons came in to experience the food.

Many of the new star chefs rising up in Los Angeles brought other values to their cooking, such as honoring food culture and diversity, preserving the environment, reducing the suffering of animals in agriculture, and moving away from indulgent, artery-clogging cuisine in pursuit of a healthier, kinder, greener way of cooking. That's why you'll see plant-centric dishes on nearly every menu in the city, whether the chef or restaurant is vegan or not. Many restaurant menus boast pages devoted to vegan options and menu options sporting "v" symbols. You'll also find a plethora of completely plant-based restaurants, and even vegan street fairs, fashion shows, pop-ups, Oktoberfest, and a beer festival. The style of vegan cuisine runs the gamut from authentic ethnic food and fast food to zen meals and elegant fare.

I can't talk about LA's food vibe without getting into the power of health as a key influencer. After all, this is the city of stars, where people come to follow their dreams to the silver screen. But it's also the city of sunshine, where people surf, skate, bike, and jog their way through the city. Angelinos want to be forever young. It's where people virtually live outside year-round, given LA's status as the city with the most pleasant weather in the country. Hence, the pedestrian paths that line neighborhoods, outdoor dining tables at restaurants, and bustling parks filled with family potlucks. It's where popular diet fads (both good and bad) are born, from juicing to cleansing to keto. The city worships fresh produce, considering California has the largest number of farmers markets and organic farms in the US. And anybody with a plot of soil likely has a fresh citrus or avocado tree or two, which thoroughly love to be spoiled by the soils and warm light of this region. So, it's only fitting that a light, kind, healthy, farm-to-table way of eating would take root and flourish here in the City of Angels.

Los Angeles has long held its arms open wide to embrace people from all over the world. It's no surprise that people from 140 different nations call this city home. With its proximity to Central America, the Pacific, and Asia, Los Angeles is a hub for people from this part of the world. And the jobs in aerospace, technology, entertainment, and fashion draw the best and brightest from every corner of the globe. This cultural diversity is stamped on the food scene, which reflects authentic, global flavors the city's denizens crave. And, oh, there are so many authentic global neighborhoods to savor in LA, including a Chinatown that dates back to 1852, Little Armenia, Olvera Street—the birthplace of Los Angeles and keeper of Mexican food traditions—Thai Town, Little Ethiopia, Historic Filipi-notown, Koreatown, Little Tokyo, Pico-Robertson's center for Orthodox Jews and kosher restaurants, and South LA's mecca for soul food. A resi-dent could stay busy for a lifetime just trying to sample all of the good food to be had in Los Angeles. I know I have been trying my best.

Tuning into the LA Plant-Based Food Vibe

You can live the La La Land life with these cooking tips:

- Infuse the simplest of dishes with global flavor, such as a sprinkle of freshly grated turmeric or ginger, and spice blends, like garam masala or za'atar.

- Think healthy indulgence—slather on the tahini ginger sauce, avocado slices, and hummus over your salads, grain dishes, and beyond.

- Combine street food with small plates when meal planning. At meal-time, enjoy several small, flavorful foods packed with flavor, such as California Grilled Street Corn (page 34), Buffalo Cauliflower with Vegan Ranch Dressing (page 41), and vegan tacos.

Green Goddess Grain Bowl

Grain bowls—light, healthy meals comprised of a whole grain, lots of vegetables, a healthful protein source, and a flavorful sauce—are all the rage in California. This bowl combines the star nutrition power of whole grain sorghum and beans with cool green veggies, such as arugula, avocados, cucumbers, asparagus, and pumpkin seeds. Plus, it's topped with a house-made, plant-based Green Goddess Dressing that is as tasty as it is pretty.

SERVES 4

2 cups cooked whole grain sorghum, cooled

1 15-ounce can white beans (Great Northern, cannellini)

1 bunch fresh asparagus, trimmed, sliced

4 cups packed baby arugula leaves

1 medium avocado, sliced

1 medium cucumber, sliced

¼ cup pumpkin seeds

Vegan Green Goddess Dressing (page 29)

Cook whole grain sorghum to make 2 cups, according to package directions, and cool, draining any remaining liquid.

Rinse and drain white beans and set aside.

Blanch asparagus by cooking it in boiling water for 3–4 minutes, until tender, but bright green; set aside.

Arrange 1 cup arugula leaves at the bottom of each of four large, individual serving bowls.

Arrange over the arugula leaves in each bowl:

one fourth of the white beans (about ½ cup).

½ cup cooked, cooled sorghum.

one fourth of the sliced avocado.

one fourth of the cucumber slices (about ½ cup).

one fourth of the blanched, cooled asparagus.

A dollop (about 2 tablespoons) of Green Goddess Dressing.

Sprinkle with 1 tablespoon pumpkin seeds.

Serve immediately.

Nutrition information per serving (1 bowl): 393 calories, 9 g total fat, 1 g saturated fat, 0 mg cholesterol, 20 mg sodium, 69 g carbohydrates, 18 g fiber, 4 g sugar, 18 g protein

Vegan Green Goddess Dressing

SERVES 4

1½ tablespoons plant-based milk, plain, unsweetened

¼ ripe large avocado, peeled, sliced

¼ cup diced cucumber, with peel

3 tablespoons chopped fresh herbs (dill, parsley, oregano, basil, thyme, cilantro)

1 stalk green onion, white and green parts, diced

1 small garlic clove

Pinch white pepper

2 tablespoons lemon juice, freshly squeezed

Place all of the ingredients into the container of a small blender and process until smooth.

Place in an airtight container and refrigerate until serving time.

Makes ½ cup per serving.

Nutrition information per serving: 21 calories, 1 g total fat, 0 g saturated fat, 0 mg cholesterol, 4 mg sodium, 2 g carbohydrates, 1 g fiber, 0.5 g sugar, 0.5 g protein

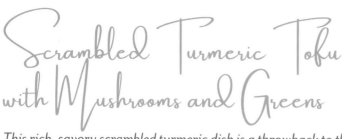

Scrambled Turmeric Tofu with Mushrooms and Greens

This rich, savory scrambled turmeric dish is a throwback to the golden hippy days of earthy, satisfying plant-based meals based on tofu, turmeric, and nutritional yeast, long before they became mainstays in every supermarket. With a touch of nutritious greens and sun-dried tomatoes, this hearty scramble can go from breakfast to dinner easily.

SERVES 6

1 15-ounce package extra firm tofu, pressed (see *Note*)

2 tablespoons nutritional yeast

2 teaspoons turmeric

½ teaspoon smoked paprika

¼ teaspoon black pepper

Pinch sea salt (optional)

2 tablespoons plant-based milk, plain, unsweetened

1 tablespoon extra-virgin olive oil

1 scallion, finely diced

2 cloves garlic, minced

6 ounces (about 2¼ cups) sliced brown mushrooms

2 cups loosely packed chopped greens (mustard, collard, spinach, kale)

¼ cup sun-dried tomatoes, chopped

Press tofu and drain off extra liquid.

Place tofu in a bowl and break up with a fork to achieve a crumbly texture. Mix in nutritional yeast, turmeric, smoked paprika, black pepper, salt (optional), and plant-based milk.

Heat olive oil in a skillet and sauté scallion, garlic, and mushrooms for about 5 minutes.

Add tofu, chopped greens, and sun-dried tomatoes and sauté just until greens start to wilt. Serve immediately. May serve with sliced avocados, if desired

Note: One easy way to press tofu is to simply wrap it in several sheets of paper towels, sandwich it in between two plates, and then anchor it down with something heavy (like a book) for 15 minutes or so. Sometimes it's easy to consider pressing tofu to be a bothersome task. Fortunately, with the increased interest in tofu, tofu presses are now available, which makes pressing tofu a bit easier. I have a couple of different types of tofu presses and they work fairly similarly—you just put the tofu in the device, apply pressure through the device's crank, let it sit for several minutes to let the liquid drain off, and remove the tofu.

Nutrition information per serving: 152 calories, 9 g total fat, 1 g saturated fat, 0 mg cholesterol, 71 mg sodium, 8 g carbohydrates, 3 g fiber, 0 g sugar, 14 g protein

Fava Bean Asparagus Sauté

Nothing spells spring comfort quite like the first appearance of both asparagus and fava beans in farmers markets. These cool, verdant veggies emerge from the warm, damp earth and on plush vines during the first warm days of spring. In fact, I have both of these lovely veggies gracing my vegetable garden. This easy spring Fava Bean Asparagus Sauté showcases these vegetables to their very best ability in a simple, straightforward dish, which can be enjoyed as an entrée or side dish or served over grains or pasta. Nothing too fussy or complicated—just let the natural ingredients shine through.

SERVES 6

1½ tablespoons extra-virgin olive oil (may use more for garnish)

2 pounds fresh fava beans (in the shell), about 2 cups shelled (may use frozen)

1 pound fresh asparagus, trimmed, chopped into 2–3-inch pieces (may use frozen)

2 spring onions, sliced (tops and bulb)

2 garlic cloves, minced

1 lemon, juiced, zested

¼ cup fresh mint leaves, chopped coarsely

¼ cup fresh basil leaves, chopped coarsely

Sea salt and black pepper, to taste (optional)

Heat olive oil in a large saucepan or skillet.

Sauté fava beans, asparagus, onions, and garlic for about 6–7 minutes, until veggies are crisp tender, yet bright green and not overcooked.

Remove from heat and toss in lemon juice and lemon zest, mint, and basil leaves. Season with salt and pepper if desired.

Serve immediately.

Nutrition information per serving: 221 calories, 4 g total fat, 1 g saturated fat, 10 mg sodium, 0 mg cholesterol, 34 g carbohydrates, 14 g fiber, 5 g sugar, 15 g protein

California Grilled Street Corn

Street corn is the stuff of substance in countless Central and South American villages. Of course! The husks from the hearty ears of corn were peeled back, creating a sort of "handle," and then they were simply and lovingly grilled by a vendor on a portable cart, after which they were slathered with local fresh cheese, herbs, and spices. That would be enough nutrition to keep you going for a few hours, with minimal cost. That tradition is alive and well in the streets of LA, too. I took this rustic ritual and gave it a plant-based update with my Almond Cilantro Cotija (page 37)—a freshly made dry, herb-filled almond cheese. This dish is so satisfying, it can be the true star of your own street food scene!

SERVES 4

For the corn:

4 ears of corn

½ tablespoon extra-virgin olive oil

For the sauce:

¼ cup plant-based, light mayonnaise

¼ cup plant-based sour cream

1 jalapeño, finely diced

¼ teaspoon chili powder

1 lime, juiced

⅓ cup Almond Cilantro Cotija (page 37)

Preheat grill to high setting.

Peel away the outer leaves of the ears of corn without completely removing them from the ear of corn. Clean silk from ears of corn. Gather the leaves together in a bunch at the base of the corn, and use one leaf to secure the leaves together into a knot (see photo).

Brush the ears of corn with the olive oil and grill on high, turning occasionally, until tender and golden brown (about 15 minutes). Remove from grill and place on a platter.

While corn is grilling, prepare the sauce by mixing together plant-based mayo and sour cream, jalapeño, chili powder, and lime juice in a dish.

Prepare ⅓ cup of the Almond Cilantro Cotija.

Slather the sauce evenly over the corn, then sprinkle with the cotija. Serve on a platter or individually, using the leaves as a holder for the corn.

Nutrition information per serving: 266 calories, 17 g total fat, 3 g saturated fat, 110 mg sodium, 0 mg cholesterol, 24.5 g carbohydrates, 4 g fiber, 4 g sugar, 8 g protein

 Almond Cilantro Cotija

Plant-based cheeses are easy to whip up on your own. The dry, crumbly Mexican dairy-based cotija cheese can be reproduced easily in a plant-based version starring almonds. Just toss almonds, garlic, nutritional yeast, and cilantro into a blender, food processor, or food chopper, and grind until crumbly.

SERVES 4

⅓ cup almonds, peeled, slivered

1 tablespoon nutritional yeast

1 clove garlic

¼ teaspoon salt (optional)

2 tablespoons finely chopped cilantro

Place almonds, nutritional yeast, garlic, and salt (optional) into the container of a food processor, chopper, or blender.

Grind until it achieves a fine, sandy-grainy texture, without turning into a paste.

Remove from processor or blender and transfer to a small dish. Mix in chopped cilantro.

Makes about ⅓ cup.

Nutrition information per serving: 59 calories, 5 g total fat, 0 g saturated fat, 0 mg cholesterol, 1 mg sodium, 3 g carbohydrates, 1 g sugar, 2 g fiber, 3 g protein

Peach Rosemary Olive Oil Crisp

California has a pure Mediterranean spirit that shines right through in simple fruit-forward desserts, like this crisp made of perfectly ripe, farm-fresh peaches. The crunchy oat crust is infused with California extra-virgin olive oil and rosemary—which grows with abandon in sunny gardens, like my own.

SERVES 8

For the peach filling:

8 fresh large peaches, peeled, sliced

1 tablespoon coconut palm sugar (or brown sugar)

1½ teaspoons fresh rosemary, chopped

1 lemon (juice and zest)

3 tablespoons orange juice

For the crisp topping:

1 cup old-fashioned oats

¼ cup all-purpose flour

½ teaspoon vanilla

¼ cup extra-virgin olive oil (preferably Californian)

½ teaspoon cinnamon

Pinch kosher salt

1½ tablespoons coconut palm sugar (or brown sugar)

For the garnish:

Fresh rosemary sprigs, as desired

Preheat oven to 375°F.

To make the peach filling: In a medium bowl, mix together peaches, coconut palm sugar (or brown sugar), rosemary, lemon juice and zest, and orange juice until well combined. Place in a 9 × 13-inch baking dish or divide among eight individual small baking dishes (soufflé cups).

To make the crisp topping: In a small bowl, mix together oats, flour, vanilla, olive oil, cinnamon, salt, and coconut palm sugar (or brown sugar) to make a crumbly topping. Sprinkle over the peach mixture in the baking dish or individual dishes.

Place peach crisp in the oven, uncovered, and bake 40–45 minutes, until golden brown and tender.

Remove from oven, garnish with rosemary sprigs, and serve immediately.

Nutrition information per serving: 222 calories, 9 g fat, 1 g sat fat, 0 mg cholesterol, 1 mg sodium, 34 g carbohydrates, 5 g dietary fiber, 16 g sugar, 5 g protein

Buffalo Cauliflower with Vegan Ranch Dressing

I am not positive, but I think the buffalo cauliflower trend might have taken root in LA. The first time I got a whiff of this delectable appetizer was at a funky little old bowling alley turned restaurant in Silver Lake. Who would ever have thought that cauliflower could take the place of chicken wings so gracefully? Indeed, a food trend was born. I will tell you, though, that many versions of this addictive dish—crispy cauliflower with a spicy-rich batter, served with ranch—are weighed down with fat, thanks to a trip to the deep fryer. This baked version is a lot lighter in fat, and comes with my own classic, light, herbal Vegan Ranch Dressing (page 42) on the side, plus a complement of crunchy celery sticks.

SERVES 8

2 medium heads cauliflower, split into florets

1 cup flour (use gluten-free flour, such as sorghum or rice to make this recipe gluten-free)

¾ teaspoon garlic powder

1 teaspoon paprika

½ teaspoon salt (optional)

1 cup water

2 teaspoons white vinegar

2 tablespoons extra-virgin olive oil

2–4 tablespoons hot sauce (based on your preference for spiciness)

2 tablespoons sweet chili sauce or ketchup

1 cup Vegan Ranch Dressing (page 42)

Celery sticks

Preheat oven to 450°F.

Spray a baking sheet with nonstick cooking spray and set aside.

In a medium bowl, mix together flour, garlic powder, paprika, and salt (optional). Stir in water, vinegar, olive oil, hot sauce, and chili sauce or ketchup until smooth to make a batter.

Dip the cauliflower florets into the batter and arrange evenly on the baking sheet. Drizzle any remaining batter over the cauliflower florets.

Place in top shelf of oven and roast for 25–30 minutes, until golden brown and tender.

Place the Vegan Ranch Dressing in a serving bowl, arrange hot cauliflower on a platter, and serve with celery sticks on the side.

Nutrition information per serving: 170 calories, 8 g total fat, 1 g saturated fat, 0 mg cholesterol, 369 mg sodium, 23 g carbohydrates, 4 g fiber, 5 g sugar, 4 g protein

Vegan Ranch Dressing

There's nothing like a cool, creamy, herbal ranch dressing to accompany a crisp salad, fresh veggie platter, or buffalo cauliflower recipe. And you can whip up a vegan batch in no time! Try this easy, breezy Vegan Ranch Dressing and store it in the fridge for up to one week to serve with your favorite dishes all week long.

SERVES 8

½ cup vegan light mayonnaise

⅓ cup plant-based milk, plain, unsweetened

1 teaspoon white vinegar

1 clove garlic, minced

3 tablespoons assorted freshly chopped herbs (dill, basil, oregano, chives, parsley, cilantro, tarragon)

¼ teaspoon paprika

Pinch salt (optional)

Mix all ingredients together in a small bowl until smooth.

Store in a covered container in the refrigerator for up to one week.

Serve with your favorite dishes, such as salads, veggie platters, veggie balls, or roasted vegetables.

Makes 1 cup (2 tablespoons per serving).

Nutrition information per serving: 41 calories, 4 g total fat, 0 g saturated fat, 115 mg sodium, 2 g carbohydrates, 0 g sugar, 0 g protein

3

Indigenous Food Traditions

The region we call California today was a veritable land of bounty for the indigenous peoples, observed the first European explorers to the area. Unlike other nomadic Native American tribes in other regions of the Americas, who traveled in tune with the food supply and weather, the tribes in California could afford to build huts and stay put. They didn't even have to rely heavily upon agriculture, such was the abundance of wild food.

Wild grasses line a field in Ojai beneath a majestic California Live Oak, the iconic evergreen oak native to California.

Long, long ago, when California arose from its slumber beneath a warm sea bath during the Paleozoic, plants started emerging, evolving and adapting to the climatic and geographic influences. The mountains pushed up, the valleys were flooded and filled with sediment, and rich ecosystems, such as grassland, woodland, coastal, and chaparral, took hold in California—each offering generous food supplies.

The first humans to arrive to the Americas were those rugged early adventurers who walked over the Bering land bridge, eventually making their way to California some 10,000 to 40,000 years ago. Though there were many tribes that made their homes across the 164,000 square miles of modern-day California, in the scrubby hills overlooking Los Angeles the Tongva tribe feasted on acorns (a staple from the native live oak trees), pine nuts, herbs, berries, mushrooms, flowering plants, bulbs, seeds, leaves, stems, tubers, and roots from the forest. Other coastal tribes, like the Chumash, added seaweed and sea vegetables to their diets. The plants were gathered and stored, providing a major source of nutrition. Acorns were pounded into flour to make a soup or mush, which was cooked over an open fire in a stone pot, or hot stones were added to baskets with water and acorn meal.

The native tribes also learned to practice the poly-agricultural tradition, the "Three Sisters"—maize, beans, and squash—as the cornerstone of their diet. They planted maize (corn) on a mound, with a bean vine at its base, which would trail up the stalk using it as a beanpole, while also providing nitrogen to the soil. Squash was also planted at the base to provide a shady canopy to preserve moisture and nutrients in the soil. The first people lived in harmony with their environment, taking only enough to survive. Depending upon foraging and careful plantings, they were able to live healthfully and peacefully in this abundant land.

Many of our most beloved foods around the world originated in the Americas, tended to by the hands of these early peoples, including avocados, cacao, corn, chia, potatoes, tomatoes, peppers, squash, and sunflowers. The Spanish explorers brought these incredible foods with them from the New World to the Old World, where they traveled from country to country, becoming an important part of each food culture along the way.

Explore Indigenous Foods and Traditions

Here are a few ways you can honor native traditions in your own bioregion.

- Search out a few indigenous food traditions in your region. Maybe there is a traditional recipe, based on native foods, that can be traced back in time.

- Look for historically cultivated and even indigenous foods that come from your area. From mushrooms to herbs to nuts, many precious foods have been used throughout history for wellness.

- Think about the history of food the next time you go shopping—consider how long that plant has evolved, how it was treasured for sustenance by peoples before us, and how it contributes to vital health in so many ways.

Desert Sage Lentils

This dish celebrates the simplicity and beauty of slow-simmered lentils, rich in protein and fiber. One variety of lentils called Desert Sage is essentially a house blend of lentils, including green and white varieties. Indeed, these lentils create a lovely, subtle silver-green color reminiscent of the scrubby chaparral hills of Southern California, where the Tongva tribe once lived in peaceful balance with their environs. This recipe can utilize any type of lentils, however, in addition to sage—another ingredient that grows wild in those hills. Just sauté onions and garlic with a few key herbs and spices, add lentils and broth, and let it simmer away. Soon, you'll have dinner on the table in under thirty minutes with eight ingredients (not including pantry staples).

SERVES 6

1 teaspoon extra-virgin
  olive oil

½ medium yellow onion,
  chopped

2 cloves garlic, minced

2 teaspoons dried sage
  (or fresh)

½ teaspoon dried, ground
  mustard

1 tablespoon whole grain
  prepared mustard

½ teaspoon cayenne pepper

Pinch salt (optional)

2 cups Desert Sage Lentils
  blend (or a variety of
  green, brown, and white
  lentils)

4 cups vegetable broth

Heat oil in a medium pot.

Add onions and garlic and sauté for 4 minutes.

Add sage, dried mustard, whole grain mustard, cayenne pepper, and salt (optional) and sauté for 1 minute. Add lentils and vegetable broth. Stir well, cover, and bring to a boil. Simmer for about 20–25 minutes, until lentils are tender yet firm.

Taste and adjust cayenne pepper and salt as needed. Serve immediately.

Nutrition information per serving: 101 calories, 1 g total fat, 0 g saturated fat, 0 mg cholesterol, 331 mg sodium, 36 g carbohydrates, 6 g fiber, 3 g sugar, 7 g protein

Three Sisters Chili

Here's a history and sustainability lesson all wrapped up with your next meal. This delicious, healthy chili is inspired by the story of the "Three Sisters," a Native American agricultural tradition of planting beans, squash, and maize (corn) together. This planting style was practiced by the indigenous peoples of the Americas dating back to AD 1000. The corn was planted in a mound, a bean was planted at the base, using the corn as a pole, and the squash created a canopy, controlling sun exposure and soil moisture levels. This system also helped achieve biological interactions among pests and weeds, and contributed nitrogen to the soil through the cultivation of legumes. The Native Americans really knew something about sustainability! There was also enormous nutritional value in the pairing of these nutrient-rich foods: legumes, grains, and vegetables.

The Native Americans also had a bounty of indigenous herbs and spices at their fingertips, which they used in cooking, including bay leaves, juniper berries, tarragon, mint, and chilies. I included all of these spices in my Three Sisters Chili, along with tomatoes and bell peppers (both originating in the Americas).

SERVES 10

1 pound red beans (kidney, small red, cranberry), dried

7 cups water

1 vegetable bouillon cube

1 small acorn squash, peeled, cubed (about 2¼ cups)

1 onion, diced

3 cloves garlic, minced

3 stalks celery, diced

1 bell pepper, diced

3 bay leaves

1 teaspoon juniper berries, ground (available at spice shops or online)

2 teaspoons ground, dried sage

½–1 teaspoon crushed red chili pepper (according to taste preference)

1 teaspoon dried tarragon

1 cup frozen corn

1 cup tomato sauce

1 6-ounce can tomato paste

2 tablespoons fresh mint, chopped

Sea salt (optional)

Fresh tarragon and sage, if desired

Soak beans overnight in water.

Drain and place beans in a large pot. Add fresh water (7 cups), vegetable bouillon cube, squash, onion, garlic, celery, pepper, bay leaves, juniper berries, sage, chili pepper, tarragon, and corn. Stir well, cover, and bring to a boil. Simmer over medium-low for 1 hour, stirring occasionally. May need to replace water lost to evaporation.

Add tomato sauce and tomato paste. Cook for an additional 15–30 minutes, until thick and beans are tender. Add fresh mint and stir well. Remove bay leaves. Season with salt (optional). May serve with fresh tarragon and sage, if desired.

Nutrition information per serving: 216 calories, 9 g sugar, 233 mg sodium, 1 g fat, 0 g saturated fat, 43 g total carbohydrates, 6 g fiber, 5 g sugar, 6 g protein

Summer Succotash Sage Salad

The hearty combination of corn and beans in a thick stew-like dish was a cornerstone of Native American diets. In fact, legend has it that the word "succotash" comes from a Wampanoag word for "boiled corn kernels." This recipe pays homage to those smart food traditions that formed the basis for survival of both people and ecosystems in California. Today, the dish gets a modern reinvention as a chilled salad, featuring lima beans, corn, bell peppers, onions, celery, tomatoes, and jalapeños, with a sage vinaigrette.

SERVES 6

For the salad:

2 small ears fresh corn, cooked, cooled, shucked (or 2 cups frozen, thawed corn)

2 cups frozen lima beans, thawed

1 small red bell pepper, chopped

3 green onions, sliced

2 stalks celery, sliced

1 cup cherry tomatoes, halved

½ small jalapeño pepper, finely diced

For the sage vinaigrette:

1½ tablespoons extra-virgin olive oil

2 tablespoons red wine vinegar

1 clove garlic, minced

2 tablespoons fresh sage, chopped (or 1 tablespoon dried)

Salt and pepper (to taste)

In a large bowl, mix together corn, lima beans, bell pepper, green onions, celery, tomatoes, and jalapeño.

In a small dish, whisk together olive oil, vinegar, garlic, sage, salt and black pepper (to taste). Toss into succotash mixture.

Nutrition information per serving: 126 calories, 4 g total fat, 0.5 g saturated fat, 56 mg sodium, 0 mg cholesterol, 19 g carbohydrates, 5 g fiber, 3 g sugar, 5 g protein

New World Potato Avocado Salad

The humble, ubiquitous potato originated in Peru, where today there are literally thousands of colorful varieties. Around the same time, avocados originated in south central Mexico. Add tomatoes, which originated in Central America, to the lot, and you'll observe that three of the most beloved plant foods on the planet originated in the New World. The Spanish colonists saw the potential in these beauties, and introduced them to Europe, Asia, and North Africa, and the rest is history. These American foods are treasured in a fresh, California take on a classic potato salad featured with a lemon vinaigrette.

SERVES 8

For the salad:

1 pound small multi-colored potatoes, unpeeled

2 medium avocados, ripe, diced

½ bell pepper, thinly sliced

¼ red onion, thinly sliced

1 cup cherry tomatoes, sliced in half

½ cup chopped cilantro

For the lemon vinaigrette:

1 lemon, juiced

2 tablespoons extra-virgin olive oil

1 clove garlic, minced

¼ teaspoon black pepper

Sea salt (optional)

Place potatoes in a medium pot, cover with water, cover with a lid, and bring to a boil.

Cook until just tender, but firm (about 15–20 minutes). Allow to cool, then slice into chunks.

Place potatoes, avocado, bell pepper, onion, tomatoes, and cilantro into a medium bowl. Toss gently together.

To make the lemon vinaigrette: Mix lemon juice, olive oil, garlic, pepper, and sea salt (as desired) in a small dish and pour over salad, gently mixing in to moisten salad.

Serve at room temperature, or chill until serving time.

Nutrition information per serving: 162 calories, 11 g total fat, 1.5 g saturated fat, 9 mg sodium, 0 mg cholesterol, 17 g carbohydrates, 6 g fiber, 1.5 g sugar, 2.5 g protein

Andean Quinoa Bean Chowder

Plant-based food traditions abound in the Sacred Valley of Peru, where countless plant foods originated and still thrive today in the nutrient-rich soils of the valley where small farms still dot the landscape. The three classic staples of this region include quinoa, beans, and corn—the backbone of healthful, indigenous plant-based diets from the Americas, including the first people who lived in the land of bounty that became known as California. In rural villages of the Americas, where diets have changed little over the centuries, rates of chronic disease and obesity are low, compared to the cities where diets have gradually grown to resemble the Standard American Diet (SAD). Take a lesson from the history books with this delicious, satisfying chowder.

SERVES 6

1 cup quinoa, uncooked (red, white, or multi-colored)

1 tablespoon extra-virgin olive oil

1 onion, chopped

1 bell pepper, chopped (red, green, yellow, or orange)

2 garlic cloves, minced

4 cups vegetable broth

2 cups plain, unsweetened plant-based milk (soy or almond)

2 cups frozen sweet corn, thawed

1 15-ounce can pinto beans, drained (may substitute black beans)

2 tablespoons chopped fresh parsley

1 teaspoon dried thyme

½ teaspoon cayenne pepper

Pinch salt (optional)

Heat a heavy pot and toast quinoa in the pot for 1 minute, stirring frequently.

Add olive oil, onions, bell pepper, and garlic and sauté for 3–4 minutes.

Add broth and plant-based milk, stirring well.

Add corn, beans, parsley, thyme, cayenne pepper, and salt (optional). Stir until well combined.

Heat chowder, stirring frequently, until bubbly and thickened, and quinoa and vegetables are tender—about 10–15 minutes.

Pour into bowls and serve immediately.

Nutrition information per serving: 282 calories, 6 g total fat, 1 g saturated fat, 46 g carbohydrates, 10 g fiber, 3 g sugar, 12 g protein, 252 mg sodium

4

Loma Linda, Home of the Blue Zones

As a young nutrition student at Loma Linda University, I took for granted that my health education was based solely on plants, and that the hospital served no meat (unless you received a doctor's order for it, and it was prepared in a "quarantined" kitchen). After all, it pretty much matched my own upbringing. This community of Loma Linda, California, was home to a throng of Seventh-Day Adventists, a Christian religion that was also the founder of Loma Linda University. Their beliefs include several diet and health principles, such as abstinence from alcohol, coffee, and tobacco and avoidance of specific animal foods, with an overall goal of eating a vegetarian-style diet. Hence, there are a lot of vegans and vegetarians in the Seventh-Day Adventist faith, as well as in the Loma Linda community.

Thirty years ago, we didn't know much about the health benefits that soon would be established in the very same university, by way of the Adventist Health Studies—pioneering nutrition research that would go on to compare the health outcomes of thousands and thousands of people, based upon diet pattern. Still regarded as the holy grail for plant-based nutrition research around the world, the Adventist Health Studies were among the first scientific studies to establish that plant-based diets—vegan, vegetarian, semi-vegetarian, and pescatarian—were not only risk-free, but actually beneficial. It's hard to believe, but at that time the health community counselled against plant-based diets for fear that they would cause nutrient deficiencies. Yet, the research from Loma Linda would go on to link plant-based diet patterns with lower risks of obesity and chronic diseases, pointing out that the more plant-based your diet, generally the better the health outcome. Their data also linked vegans with a 42% lower carbon footprint than non-vegetarians.

Around the same time another concept was brewing: the Blue Zones. *National Geographic* journalist Dan Buettner was on assignment, studying places around the world where people live the longest. He found five "Blue Zones" on the planet—places with the largest concentrations of centenarians (living to at least 100 years of age). They were located in Japan, Greece, Italy, and Costa Rica, with one in the US. Where was that one Blue Zone located, among all of the cities in the US? You guessed it! The small college town of Loma Linda, where many people eat a vegetarian or vegan diet.

One such Loma Linda centenarian, as well as personal friend, Dr. Ellsworth Wareham, became the literal face of the Blue Zone movement. Dr. Wareham was a noted thoracic surgeon and pioneer of heart surgery, traveling around the world to teach other universities how to save lives with these procedures. Yet, he found that diet was more powerful than the knife when it came to preventing heart disease—the number one killer in the US. Dr. Wareham was a regular guest in the media on the topic of the Blue Zones. Dr. Sanjay Gupta interviewed him on CNN (check it out on YouTube), where Dr. Wareham shared his style of eating and showed how he could still mow the lawn and do pretty much anything he wanted at the ripe age of 100. Dr. Wareham only recently passed away at the age of 104. Remarkable!

What are the lessons of the Blue Zones? Buettner found that all five of these communities had several things in common: They ate a primarily plant-based diet, they exercised regularly (and not by going to the gym), and they had strong social support systems. All of these are on full display in Loma Linda. The Blue Zones discovered that diet was just one facet to long life—it was also about going for a walk after dinner, finding meaning in life, and never leaving those we love in isolation. These are things we should aspire to within the plant-based community—to offer hope and support to those in our own regions. The Blue Zones Project is moving forward, working to set up new Blue Zones communities based on these principles.

So, what do people eat in this sunny spot in the hills of San Bernardino County—halfway between Los Angeles and the desert? Well, the Seventh-Day Adventist community has been eating plant-based for a long time. Thus, a sort of kitschy food culture has arisen, with recipes being handed around at potlucks, prayer meetings, and get-togethers. These dishes are humble and comforting—like a soft, well-worn T-shirt you slide on when you've got the blues. Some are a bit indulgent—with a twist of "health" woven in; others were created to help people figure out what to put on their plate instead of a slab of meat, a way of eating so popular throughout the timeline of American cuisine. These recipes offer a historical glimpse of the way people have been eating a plant-based diet for the past century.

Cooking Up Classic Kitschy Plant-Based Foods in Your Kitchen

Let the Blue Zones give you guidance on eating a plant-based diet that looks beyond what you put on your fork—it's about community, support, and downright love.

- Dig up some vintage vegetarian and vegan recipe books for a flashback in time, and new, comforting ideas for cooking up plant-based meals.

- Volunteer in your local community to provide support around healthy, plant-based meals for seniors, such as Meals on Wheels, Blue Zones, or your local senior center.

- Take an old recipe from your mother or grandmother and plant-ify it. Take out the meat, but keep in the love.

Classic Haystacks (Vegetarian Chili with Corn Chip Salad) with Vegan Ranch Dressing

Have you ever heard of a "haystack"? This funky, comfort food classic was a vegetarian mainstay when I was a kid growing up veggie. It was a simple concoction: layers of crisp corn chips, vegetarian chili, cheese, lettuce, and tomatoes—with a thick dollop of ketchup. We used to just love "haystack" day at my plant-based boarding school during my high school years. To this day, it's a favorite among the Blue Zones set in Loma Linda. And in this quick five minute version, I have made it completely vegan and just a tad bit healthier. Try it for your perfect, interactive easy lunch or dinner on a busy night.

SERVES 4

1 14.5-ounce can vegetarian/vegan chili, prepared

4 ounces corn chips

4 cups chopped iceberg lettuce

2 small tomatoes, diced

¼ white onion, diced

1 cup shredded plant-based cheese

½ cup fresh cilantro, chopped

16 black olives, drained

½ cup medium salsa

½ cup Vegan Ranch Dressing (page 42)

Place vegetarian chili in a small pot to heat.

While beans are heating, assemble all toppings, including corn chips, chopped iceberg lettuce, diced tomatoes, diced onions, plant-based cheese, chopped cilantro, black olives, salsa, and Vegan Ranch Dressing.

To prepare each haystack (four servings per recipe):

Line each dinner plate with 1 ounce corn chips.

Top with ½ cup chili, 1 cup iceberg lettuce, one-fourth of the tomato (about ¼ cup each), one-fourth of the onion (about 1 tablespoon each).

Sprinkle with ¼ cup plant-based cheese and 2 tablespoons chopped cilantro; top with four olives.

Drizzle with 2 tablespoons salsa and 2 tablespoons Vegan Ranch Dressing.

Serve immediately.

Note: You can also place all toppings on a large divided platter and in individual containers for people to make their own haystack the way they prefer.

Nutrition information per serving: 377 calories, 15 g total fat, 2 g saturated fat, 0 mg cholesterol, 1016 mg sodium, 51 g carbohydrates, 13 g sugar, 8 g fiber, 12 g protein

Herbed Lentil Patties

A heartfelt, humble lentil patty with a creamy, plant-based sauce was the stuff of family meals and potlucks of my childhood. In the Blue Zones, home cooks created cherished meals out of lentils and beans long before it was cool and trendy. Cook up a pot of lentils, mash them with sautéed veggies and herbs, shape them into patties, fry or bake them, and voila—a nourishing, satisfying meal for the whole family. These kitschy recipes may seem quaint, but they are really, really good. Try making this recipe for your next holiday dinner table, as it impresses beyond a simple weeknight meal. You'll even have non-vegheads dishing them up! I love to serve this dish with mashed potatoes and Savory Mushroom Sauce (page 64) as a perfect accompaniment.

SERVES 8

1 cup (8 ounces) small green lentils, dry

¼ cup (about 2 ounces) quinoa, dry

3 cups vegetable broth, reduced sodium

¼ cup ground flaxseeds

1 medium carrot, shredded finely

3 green onions, chopped finely

¼ cup chopped basil

2 cloves garlic, minced

½ cup old-fashioned oats, dry

1 teaspoon oregano

½ teaspoon black pepper

Salt (optional)

1 tablespoon whole grain mustard

1 tablespoon soy sauce

1 tablespoon red wine vinegar

2½ cups Savory Mushroom Sauce (page 64)

Place lentils and quinoa in a small pot and add broth. Cover and simmer over medium heat about 25 minutes, stirring occasionally, until very tender.

Drain any leftover liquid and transfer cooked lentils and quinoa to a bowl and mash slightly.

Add flaxseeds, carrot, onions, basil, garlic, oats, oregano, black pepper, and salt (if desired) to bowl with lentils and quinoa and mix well. Add mustard, soy sauce, and vinegar and stir well to moisten all ingredients. Chill for 1 hour.

Preheat oven to 375°F. Spray a baking sheet with nonstick cooking spray. Press lentil patty mixture into a ½-cup measuring cup, place onto the baking sheet, and flatten to create firm, round patties about ½ inch thick. Form eight patties with mixture.

Place in oven on top rack and bake for about 40 minutes, until golden and firm. Remove and serve with Savory Mushroom Sauce (about 3 tablespoons per patty).

Nutrition information per serving (1 patty + 5 tablespoons sauce): 212 calories, 5 g total fat, 0 g saturated fat, 0 mg cholesterol, 223 mg sodium, 32 g carbohydrates, 2 g sugar, 11 g fiber, 12 g protein

Savory Mushroom Sauce

Whip up this classic, Savory Mushroom Sauce to grace your next batch of lentil patties, mashed potatoes, biscuits, and beyond. Sautéed mushrooms and garlic are the foundation of this creamy sauce, which also includes plant-based milk. This recipe is great for a Sunday night dinner, or even your holiday table.

SERVES 8

1 teaspoon extra-virgin olive oil

¾ cup diced mushrooms

1 medium clove garlic, minced

2 cups plant-based milk, unsweetened, plain

2 tablespoons all-purpose flour

Pinch salt (optional)

¼ teaspoon black pepper

1 tablespoon reduced sodium soy sauce

2 tablespoons chopped fresh chives (additional for garnish)

Heat olive oil over medium heat in a saucepan.

Add mushrooms and garlic and sauté for 3 minutes.

Whisk together plant-based milk, flour, salt (optional), black pepper, and soy sauce in a small dish until smooth with no lumps.

Pour mixture into saucepan and cook for about 8 minutes, until bubbly and thick.

Stir in chives.

Pour in a serving dish and garnish with additional chives, if desired.

Make 2½ cups sauce.

Nutrition information per serving: 36 calories, 2 g total fat, 0 g saturated fat, 0 mg cholesterol, 89 mg sodium, 3 g carbohydrates, 0 g sugar, 0 g fiber, 2 g protein

Whole Grain Walnut Cinnamon Rolls

Going to school in a plant-based community had its culinary perks beyond alfalfa sprouts and lentils. We enjoyed plenty of foods that were quaint and comforting, plus a bit on the indulgent side. The secret was always adding in a healthier ingredient to narrow the gap between the crave-worthy and outright healthy. Nothing personifies this style of cooking more than the Friday tradition of home-made cinnamon rolls. I could smell them baking in the school cafeteria early on Friday mornings, and grew to look forward to feasting on a massive, yeasty, fragrant roll for breakfast on those mornings, which came to be part of my liberating weekend, with a week's worth of classes behind me. Sure, you can enjoy those earnestly soul-satisfying foods like cinnamon rolls without even batting an eye when you make them vegan, fill them with whole grains and heart-healthy nuts, and lighten up the sugar and fat. This classic version is a favorite of my kids. I make a batch and count the days until they are gone.

SERVES 12

For the bread dough:

1 cup warm (110°F) plant-based milk, plain, unsweetened

¼ cup pure maple syrup

1¼-ounce package (2¼ teaspoons) rapid-rise yeast

3 tablespoons melted, dairy-free margarine

2 tablespoons flaxseeds, ground

½ teaspoon salt (optional)

2½–3 cups whole wheat flour

For the maple walnut cinnamon filling:

3 tablespoons dairy-free margarine

1 cup chopped walnuts

3 tablespoons pure maple syrup

2 teaspoons cinnamon

1 tablespoon water

In the bowl of an electric stand mixer (or use a hand-held electric mixer), gently stir together plant-based milk, maple syrup, and yeast. Let stand for 10 minutes.

Using electric mixer with dough hook attachment, mix in melted margarine and flaxseeds until smooth.

Mix in salt (optional) and 2½ cups whole wheat flour. If needed, add just enough additional whole wheat flour to make a soft, slightly sticky dough.

Continue to use the electric mixer with dough hook on medium-low for 6 minutes. (Alternatively, turn dough out on floured surface and knead by hand.)

Remove dough from mixer bowl and place in a clean large bowl sprayed with nonstick cooking spray. Place in a warm place (about 80–90°F), cover with a clean towel, and let rise for 1 hour, until about doubled in size.

While dough is rising, make maple walnut cinnamon filling: Heat dairy-free margarine in a small skillet or sauté pan and stir in walnuts, maple syrup, cinnamon, and water. Stir until melted and bubbly. Set aside.

Punch down dough and turn out onto a lightly floured surface. Using a pastry roller, roll into a rectangle about 12 × 17 inches.

For the maple topping (optional):

1 tablespoon dairy-free margarine

2 tablespoons pure maple syrup

Spread the maple walnut cinnamon filling evenly over the surface of the dough.

Tightly roll up the dough horizontally (like a burrito), so that you are left with an approximately 17-inch tube of dough.

Slice roll with a serrated knife into approximately 1½-inch slices to create twelve cinnamon rolls.

Spray a 9 × 13-inch baking dish with nonstick cooking spray, and arrange cinnamon rolls in dish, cut side down. Cover with a clean dish towel and let rise for 45 minutes.

Preheat oven to 350°F.

Place baking dish in oven, uncovered, and bake for about 35 minutes, until cooked through and slightly golden.

Remove from oven. If desired (optional), dot top of rolls with small pieces of margarine and drizzle with maple syrup.

Serve immediately.

Nutrition information per serving (with maple topping): 262 calories, 14 g total fat, 2 g saturated fat, 0 mg cholesterol, 82 mg sodium, 31 g carbohydrates, 4 g fiber, 9 g sugar, 6 g protein

Best Ever Cauliflower Lasagna

Veggie lasagna is one classic plant-based dish that certainly everyone knows and loves. It's been served in my home, and in the Blue Zones, since forever. But did you know that you can move beyond the tried and true classic ingredients of vegetable lasagna and introduce some new ingredients? In this case, cauliflower. While you might not think of cauliflower as the vegetable of choice in a classic lasagna, it does quite well, thank you very much! Not only is this under-the-radar vegetable rich in flavor, it's packed with nutrients that have been linked to cancer protection. This lasagna looks impressive, but it's deceptively simple. Just cook up a simple marinara sauce with cauliflower, onions, and bell pepper, then layer pasta with spinach, sauce, plant-based sour cream and plant-based cheese, and a topping of pine nuts. You will be rewarded with pure comfort food nirvana, thanks to this fabulous combination. It only takes about fifteen minutes to get this family-sized meal in the oven and baking away for dinner. Viva la cauliflower!

SERVES 8

For the cauliflower marinara sauce:

1 tablespoon extra-virgin olive oil

1 medium onion, chopped

1 medium red bell pepper, chopped

1 small head cauliflower, broken into small florets

2 cloves garlic, minced

2 teaspoons oregano

½ teaspoon smoked paprika

1 25-ounce jar marinara sauce

For the layers and toppings:

6 sheets (about 8 ounces) whole grain lasagna, uncooked

6 ounces fresh baby spinach leaves

½ cup plant-based sour cream

1 cup shredded plant-based cheese, mozzarella

¼ cup pine nuts

To prepare the cauliflower marinara sauce: Heat olive oil in a large sauté pan or skillet. Add onion, pepper, cauliflower, and garlic. Sauté for 8 minutes. Stir in oregano, smoked paprika, and marinara sauce and heat until bubbly.

Preheat oven to 375°F.

To prepare the lasagna: Spray a 9 × 13-inch baking dish with non-stick cooking spray. Arrange three sheets of lasagna noodles on the bottom of the dish, then top with half of the spinach (3 ounces), half of the cauliflower marinara sauce, ¼ cup of the plant-based sour cream in dollops, and ½ cup plant-based cheese. Repeat layers again. Sprinkle with pine nuts.

Cover with foil and bake for 40 minutes on top rack of oven. Remove foil and bake for an additional 10–15 minutes, until browned and cooked through.

Slice into eight squares and serve immediately.

Nutrition information per serving: 230 calories, 8 g total fat, 3 g saturated fat, 0 mg cholesterol, 409 mg sodium, 34 g carbohydrates, 6 g fiber, 8 g sugar, 9 g protein

Golden Beet Veggie Balls

Plant-based communities understand this simple truth: Cooking is all about turning something whole and real—a bunch of golden beets fresh from the soil, a handful of nuts, a sprig of rosemary—into something downright fabulous and fulfilling. These veggie balls are a creative way to turn plants into pure gold, plus offer a powerful dose of nutrition to your day. Filled with the goodness of beans, grains, vegetables, and herbs, these crispy veggie balls are packed with earthy flavors, fiber, protein, phytochemicals, and more. Serve them with an easy, plant-based almond cream flavored with cranberries and rosemary. This dish makes a great appetizer, entrée, or make-ahead meal. Just watch meat-eaters and plant-eaters alike gobble them up in no time.

SERVES 8

1 bunch fresh golden beets (about 5 medium)

1 15-ounce can cannellini beans, rinsed, drained (about 1¾ cups)

2 green onions, diced

2 cloves garlic, minced

1 cup mushrooms, finely chopped

½ cup fresh chopped parsley

½ cup finely chopped hazelnuts

¼ cup ground flaxseeds

½ cup whole wheat breadcrumbs

1 teaspoon rosemary

1 teaspoon tarragon

1 teaspoon thyme

½ teaspoon smoked paprika

¼ teaspoon black pepper

Salt, as desired (optional)

2 tablespoons reduced-sodium soy sauce

2 tablespoons tahini

1 lemon, juiced

1¼ cups Almond Rosemary Cream (page 73)

Trim beets and scrub outside surface, leaving peels on. Shred beets with food processor or box grater.

Place beans in a mixing bowl and mash slightly with a potato masher to achieve a thick mixture with some lumps.

Add beets, onions, garlic, mushrooms, parsley, hazelnuts, flaxseeds, breadcrumbs, rosemary, tarragon, thyme, smoked paprika, black pepper, and salt (optional). Mix together well.

Mix in soy sauce, tahini, and lemon juice—using hands to combine well.

Cover and refrigerate for 1 hour (or overnight).

Preheat oven to 375°F and spray a baking sheet with nonstick cooking spray.

Form twenty-four golf-ball-sized balls out of the mixture and place evenly on baking sheet.

Bake veggie balls on top rack of oven for about 40 minutes, until golden brown.

Serve with Almond Rosemary Cream (2½ tablespoons per serving).

Nutrition information per serving (3 veggie balls + 2½ tablespoons cream each): 312 calories, 16 g total fat, 2 g saturated fat, 236 mg sodium, 35 g carbohydrates, 12 g fiber, 8 g sugar, 13 g protein

Almond Rosemary Cream

Blended almonds are the foundation for a creamy, herbal dip to accompany a number of foods, from savory dishes like veggie balls and lentil patties, to cracker and veggie platters, to sandwiches and wraps. This almond cream is packed with dried cranberries and rosemary, providing an aromatic taste explosion with every dip.

SERVES 8

1 cup peeled, slivered almonds

4–6 tablespoons plant-based milk, plain, unsweetened

1 tablespoon lemon juice

1 clove garlic

¼ teaspoon freshly ground black pepper

1 tablespoon fresh, chopped rosemary

¼ cup dried cranberries

Sea salt (to taste, optional)

Place almonds in a dish and cover with water. Soak for 1 hour (or overnight).

Drain water and place soaked almonds in the container of a blender or food processor.

Add 4 tablespoons plant milk, lemon juice, garlic, and black pepper and process to make a thick, creamy dip. May need to add up to 2 tablespoons more plant milk to make a desirable texture. May also need to stop processing and scrape down sides during blending.

Transfer cream to a dish and stir in fresh rosemary, cranberries, and salt (optional).

Garnish with additional freshly ground black pepper and fresh rosemary, if desired.

Makes 1¼ cups sauce.

Nutrition information per serving (2½ tablespoons each): 87 calories, 6 g total fat, 1 g saturated fat, 6 mg sodium, 7 g carbohydrates, 2 g fiber, 4 g sugar, 3 g protein

Buckwheat Almond Pancakes with Gingered Peaches

As a child growing up plant-based, a common meal was thick, fluffy pancakes with thickened canned peaches served warm as a topping. I used to help my mom can peaches every summer to use all year long in recipes like this one. I turned to buckwheat, which has a wild, nutty flavor that accents baked goods, such as hearty pancakes, so well. In this classic whole grain pancake recipe, applesauce adds a fruity, natural sweetness to the mix, along with the crunch and nutrition power of almonds. It's a perfect start for a relaxed Saturday morning breakfast, or a school day for your busy child.

SERVES 4

For the buckwheat almond pancakes:

2 tablespoons chia seeds

½ cup applesauce, unsweetened

1¼ cups plant-based milk, plain, unsweetened

2 tablespoons vegetable oil

2 tablespoons pure maple syrup

1 teaspoon cinnamon

1 tablespoon baking powder

1 cup whole wheat flour

½ cup buckwheat flour

⅓ cup finely chopped almonds

For the gingered peach sauce:

1 15-ounce can sliced peaches, in fruit juice (reserve juice)

1 tablespoon cornstarch

¼ teaspoon ground ginger

To make the buckwheat almond pancakes: In a medium bowl, mix chia seeds with applesauce, plant-based milk, oil, and maple syrup with a whisk or electric mixer, beating well for 2 minutes. Let stand for 5 minutes.

Add cinnamon, baking powder, whole wheat flour, buckwheat flour, and almonds. Combine well, but do not over-stir.

Heat a pancake griddle over medium heat. Spray with nonstick cooking spray. Add ¼ cup of batter to griddle and spread with a spatula. Cook for about 3 minutes on each side, until golden brown and cooked through.

Repeat to make eight pancakes.

To make the gingered peach sauce: Drain the juice from the peaches into a small pot. Stir in cornstarch with a whisk until smooth with no lumps. Heat and stir until thick and bubbly. Gently fold in ginger and peach slices.

Serve two pancakes with ⅔ cup warm gingered peach sauce per serving.

Nutrition information per serving (2 pancakes + ⅔ cup gingered peach topping each): 414 calories, 15 g total fat, 1 g saturated fat, 0 mg cholesterol, 40 mg sodium, 65 g carbohydrates, 21 g sugar, 11 g fiber, 12 g protein

5

Mexican Celebrations

The destinies of Mexico and California have been intertwined since the beginning of time, really. Mexico's ancient ancestors walked over that same Bering land bridge as did the ancestors of the Tongva tribe, who inhabited the scrubby hills overlooking Los Angeles where I lived for three decades. However, the indigenous peoples of present-day Mexico were influenced early on by the Spanish colonists when they uprooted the Aztec Empire in 1521.

California also experienced its own Spanish colonial period from 1769 to 1821, when the missionaries established twenty-one California missions along the coast of Alta California (the name of the region then), rounding up the natives to work on the missions and convert them

California Live Oak dot the golden rolling hills of Carmel Valley, California—a truly California vista one can glimpse across the state.

to Catholicism, ultimately decimating their traditions, as well as populations as they fell to unfamiliar diseases. Pueblos (villages) were set up to support the missions, eventually becoming some of our biggest cities, including Los Angeles, San Diego, and San Francisco. When Mexico gained its independence from Spain in 1821, Alta California became its territory, and the region entered its Rancho period, when large plots of land were allocated to officials, friends, and family of the governors. This was a short-lived time in California's history, as the US gained the territory in 1847 during the Mexican-American War.

Aside from its history, California's food culture has always been deeply influenced by its southern neighbor. Hispanics are the largest single ethnic group in the state, with most having Mexican ancestry. Thus, the familiarity and access to really good authentic Mexican food is part of everyday life. If you don't get Mexican food every week, something seems wrong! Living in California means you have a favorite taqueria, tamale vendor, or taco food truck. And the very food we grow echoes our connection; California and Mexico share many similarities in their diverse growing conditions, thus producing some of the same foods, such as tomatoes, peppers, fruits, and avocados.

While traditional Mexican food in California has morphed into an Americanized version, with heaps of cheddar cheese, sour cream, and greasy meats on fried tortilla shells, it wasn't always that way. Before that, Mexican food traditions were founded largely upon the nutritious duo of maize and beans, with additional plant foods like peppers, chilies, salt, and chocolate flavoring the cuisine. Foods were cooked over the open flame, or wrapped in cactus or banana leaves over boiling water in a pit. Salsa, meaning a sauce, based upon tomato, tomatillo, chipotle, and avocado, was present in regional food traditions long before the Spanish arrived, as well as the practice of wrapping foods in rustic tortillas made of corn. The Spanish introduced foods like beef, pork, chicken, and rice.

Today, numerous Mexican chefs are going back to their plant-based Latin roots and introducing delicious vegan traditional foods all over California. Take Gary Huerta, of Cena Vegan, who started out by selling street food in Los Angeles, serving his custom-made, plant-based meat alternatives in Latin classics, such as burritos, tacos, and platos. Based on his fan base, Huerta launched his own brand of plant-based meats (carne asada, pollo asada, al pastor, and carnitas) in stores. I've sampled amazing vegan Mexican food from Monterey to San Diego, inspiring me to create a range of my own favorite hearty, all-out crave-worthy foods honoring these Mexican traditions.

Feasting on Addictive Mexican Food with Real Latin Roots

You don't have to live in Mexico—or California—to enjoy the beauty of real Latin-inspired food. Look at the roots of Mexican food traditions, and fold them into your own.

- Serve it with salsa. This sauce is the lifeblood of Mexican cuisine, and there are hundreds of varieties of the tomato- and chili-based sauce, from salsa roja (red sauce) to salsa cruda (raw sauce). Serve it as a condiment with a range of dishes, such as breakfast home fries, tempeh hash, and simmered beans.

- Remember the simple goodness of beans and corn. Soak pinto or black beans and cook them the next day with garlic, olive oil, and onions until they are rich and creamy. Then dip hunks of freshly cooked corn tortillas into those beans. Yes, it's just that good. (Remember the salsa.)

- Enjoy fabulous fruits for dessert, honoring the amazing diversity of plant life that originates and grows in this region, including mango, banana, citrus, sapote, soursop, guava, loquat, cherimoya, and prickly pear.

Crusty Black Bean Frijoles

Frijoles—refried beans—served with corn tortillas is an essential Mexican tradition, which calls upon the nutritious combination of beans and maize, the backbone of Central American diets throughout the ages. This powerful pairing is not only packed with essential amino acids, fiber, vitamins, minerals, and phytochemicals, it is downright satisfying and delicious. A customary way of preparing frijoles is to cook them in a skillet to achieve a crusty, golden surface, as I have done with this recipe for black bean frijoles. Add sliced cabbage and Almond Cilantro Cotija (page 37) along with corn tortillas to make this meal truly memorable.

SERVES 8

For the black beans:

1 pound black beans, dried

3 tablespoons extra-virgin olive oil, divided

1 onion, finely diced

3 cloves garlic, minced

1 jalapeño, finely diced

1 teaspoon cumin

1 teaspoon chipotle seasoning

1 teaspoon chili powder

1 cup fresh cilantro, chopped

6 cups water

1 cube vegetable bouillon

Salt, as needed

For the toppings and tortillas:

½ small head cabbage, shaved or shredded

8 6-inch soft corn tortillas, warmed

½ cup Almond Cilantro Cotija (page 37)

Place black beans in a large bowl, cover with water, and soak overnight. Drain and set aside.

In a large heavy pot or Dutch oven, heat 1 tablespoon olive oil, add onions, garlic, and jalapeño, and sauté for 4 minutes. Add cumin, chipotle seasoning, chili powder, and cilantro, and sauté for 4 minutes. Add black beans (soaked, drained), along with 6 cups water and vegetable bouillon, and stir to combine.

Cover, bring to a simmer, and cook for 2 hours, stirring occasionally, until very tender. Season as desired with salt.

Drain cooked beans, reserving liquid, and transfer to a large bowl. Mash beans with a potato masher, adding one small ladle of reserved bean liquid at a time, until you achieve a smooth, creamy texture with some residual pieces of beans remaining.

Heat remaining olive oil (2 tablespoons) over medium heat in a large cast iron skillet. Pour mashed beans and spread evenly in the hot skillet and allow to cook for about 12 minutes; do not stir. You will notice holes appear in the surface (similar to pancakes). Allow bottom surface of beans to get browned and crusty. Check edges with a spatula. Do not let it burn.

Gently loosen and fold each side into the middle (like an omelet) and remove from pan with a spatula.

Place frijoles on a serving platter. Serve with shredded cabbage, warm tortillas, and Almond Cilantro Cotija.

Nutrition information per serving: 361 calories, 10 g total fat, 1 g saturated fat, 0 mg cholesterol, 23 mg sodium, 54 g carbohydrates, 13 g fiber, 4 g sugar, 17 g protein

Tofu Mole with Brown Rice

I love the flavors of authentic Central American foods, such as this plant-based take on a traditional mole dish. There are lots of legends about the origins of mole, which may be traced back to Mexico as far back as Aztec times—it comes from the ancient word "milli" for sauce or concoction. But the truly special thing about mole is that it celebrates some of the most beautiful plant foods from this part of the world: chilies, spices, tomatoes, and pure chocolate. These foods are also rich in anti-inflammatory compounds linked with disease protection. So, eat your heart out with this plant-based recipe! The vibrant mole sauce is served over pan-sautéed tofu and brown rice for an entirely hearty, full-flavored, yet simplified recipe. The rich, creamy sauce shines with powerful flavors, making it a standout!

SERVES 8

For the brown rice:

4 cups cooked medium-grain brown rice

For the mole sauce:

1 tablespoon extra-virgin olive oil

1 medium yellow onion, chopped

3 cloves garlic, minced

½ red bell pepper, diced

2 tablespoons chili powder

1 teaspoon cumin

½ teaspoon cinnamon

1 14.5-ounce can diced tomatoes, with liquid

1 cup water

1 cube vegetable bouillon

1 4-ounce can diced green chilies, with liquid

2 tablespoons peanut butter, creamy

3 ounces dark, unsweetened, dairy-free chocolate, broken into pieces (pure Mexican unsweetened baking chocolate works well, such as Taza)

Prepare brown rice according to package directions. While this is cooking, prepare the sauce and tofu.

To make the mole sauce: Heat oil in a large skillet. Sauté onions, garlic, and bell pepper until soft (about 9 minutes). Add chili powder, cumin, and cinnamon and stir for 1 minute. Add tomatoes, water, bouillon, green chilies, peanut butter, and dark chocolate. Heat until melted and bubbling. Remove from heat and cool slightly (5 minutes). Transfer to a blender or food processor container and process on low for about 2 minutes, until very smooth. Reheat sauce if necessary before serving (should be hot).

To make the pan-fried tofu: Heat olive oil in a skillet or sauté pan. Place pressed, cubed tofu in skillet or pan and sauté for about 3 minutes, then turn over and sauté the other side for 3 minutes, until golden brown.

For the pan-fried tofu:

1 tablespoon extra-virgin olive oil

2 16-ounce packages extra firm tofu, pressed (see *Note* page 30), sliced into large cubes (12 per package)

For the garnish (optional):

Green onions, sliced

Fresh cilantro, chopped

Lime wedges

To serve: Place cooked brown rice on a large serving platter. Arrange pan-fried tofu over brown rice. Ladle warm sauce over the rice and tofu. Garnish with green onions, cilantro, and lime wedges as desired. Alternatively, serve the rice and tofu separately, with the sauce and garnishes on the side, and allow people to dish up as they prefer.

Nutrition information per serving (3 cubes tofu + ½ cup rice + ½ cup sauce per serving): 357 calories, 18 g total fat, 5 g saturated fat, 0 g cholesterol, 263 mg sodium, 18 g protein, 37 g carbohydrates, 7 g fiber, 2 g sugar

Jicama Grapefruit Salad with Basil

Citrus—lemons, limes, oranges, tangerines, pomelos, mandarins, and grapefruit—grow so well in Mexico, which is why these fruits play a key role in so many cultural food traditions there. And California also puts on a big show of citrus fruits, with their deep green, waxy foliage festooning acres and acres of orchards, as well as most backyard gardens. In combination with jicama—a native of Central America—this simple recipe glows with flavor, color, and good health. The bittersweet, succulent grapefruit paired with the crisp-juicy jicama adds just the right pizzazz to this simple salad.

SERVES 6

For the salad:

3 cups assorted greens (arugula, spinach, romaine, baby lettuce)

1 large grapefruit, peeled, sectioned, chopped in large chunks

½ medium jicama, peeled, sliced into thin strips

¼ cup fresh basil leaves, chopped

For the lemon chili vinaigrette:

1 tablespoon extra-virgin olive oil

1 tablespoon lemon juice

½ small chili pepper, finely diced

1 clove garlic, minced

½ teaspoon cumin

Pinch sea salt (optional)

Arrange greens in a salad bowl or on the bottom of a platter.

In a medium bowl, mix together grapefruit, jicama, and basil.

To make the lemon chili vinaigrette: In a small dish, whisk together olive oil, lemon juice, chili pepper, garlic, cumin, and salt (optional). Drizzle dressing over grapefruit-jicama mixture and toss together.

Pile the grapefruit-jicama mixture over salad greens and serve.

Nutrition information per serving: 73 calories, 4 g total fat, 1 g saturated fat, 0 mg cholesterol, 7 mg sodium, 10 g carbohydrates, 4 g fiber, 4 g sugar, 1 g protein

Tomatillo Salsa Verde

Lemony, crunchy tomatillos are a hallmark ingredient in traditional Mexican fare. These simple green veggies—covered with a papery husk—provide a quintessential zest to Latin sauces, such as a simple green salsa. Roast the tomatillos, then whizz them up into this fragrant salsa verde, which is simply excellent served with tortilla chips, tacos, enchiladas, and beyond.

SERVES 10

5 fresh tomatillos (about 12 ounces)

½ large onion, sliced in chunks

2 cloves garlic

½ cup fresh cilantro, stems and leaves

2 small limes, juiced

1 jalapeño pepper, halved

Salt, as desired

Preheat oven to 450°F.

Remove the husk from the tomatillos and slice them in half. Place cut side down on a small baking sheet and place on the top rack of the oven. Roast until slightly golden and soft (about 8–10 minutes).

Combine tomatillos with onion, garlic, cilantro, lime juice, and jalapeño in the container of a blender and process until smooth.

Season with salt as desired, mixing well.

Chill until serving time. Serve with chips, tacos, enchiladas, quesadillas, or tofu skewers. Store in an airtight container in the refrigerator for up to two weeks.

Makes about 2½ cups salsa (about ¼ cup per serving).

Nutrition information per serving: 12 calories, 0.2 g total fat, 0 g saturated fat, 0 mg cholesterol, 1 mg sodium, 3 g carbohydrates, 0.5 g fiber, 1 g sugar, 0.5 g protein

Orange Guacamole with Blue Corn Tortilla Chips

Avocados and citrus tend to grow together in the same regions. In fact, in many parts of California—Ojai, Santa Barbara, San Diego—you will find orchards of both fruits grown right next to each other. So, this tangy-sweet guacamole pays homage to the perfect pairing of these two ingredients—which pretty much screams the California-Latin lifestyle. Just take a classic guacamole and add fresh orange sections to the mix. Serve it with pretty blue corn tortilla chips. Get ready to impress!

SERVES 8

For the orange guacamole:

4 medium avocados, ripe

2 tablespoons fresh orange juice

1 large orange

¼ cup finely chopped white onion

½ jalapeño pepper, finely chopped

2 garlic cloves, minced

Sea salt (optional)

Pinch freshly ground black pepper

For the blue corn tortilla chips:

8-ounce bag blue corn tortilla chips

Slice each avocado in half, remove pit, and scoop out flesh with a spoon into a medium bowl.

Mash avocado flesh with a fork until smooth.

Mix in orange juice.

Use a small grater or zester to zest the orange; add to the avocado. Peel the orange with a knife and remove visible pith (white tissue surrounding orange). Slice the orange into small chunks and add to the avocado.

Add white onion, jalapeño, and garlic to avocado, stirring well.

Season with sea salt (as desired) and freshly ground black pepper.

Serve with blue corn tortilla chips.

Makes about 2 cups of guacamole (¼ cup guacamole with 1 ounce chips per serving)

Nutrition information per serving: 318 calories, 21 g total fat, 3 g saturated fat, 12 mg sodium, 31 g carbohydrates, 9 g fiber, 4 g sugar, 5 g protein

6

Farmers Market Sojourn

Relax for an hour over a weekend cup of coffee, buckwheat pancakes (page 74), and the paper, preferably sitting outside in the dappled morning sun. Then it's off to the farmers market for a pleasurable stroll among stands that offer colorful produce, samplings of strawberries, chats with farmers, artisanal crafted foods, and live music. At the Ojai farmers market, they even offer "free hugs." This is a perfect way to spend the day, in my mind, and thousands upon thousands of farmers market patrons in California might agree.

It only makes sense that farmers markets would be a thing in California, which is the veritable golden land of agriculture, producing some of the world's most treasured delicacies, including olives, lemons, pistachios, and grapes. A total of 77,500 farms and ranches produce more than 400 commodities worth $47 billion, making up over a third of the country's vegetable production and two-thirds of its fruits and nuts. No wonder California is the leading agricultural state in the US.

Locally grown, colorful radishes and spring onions in every shade of pink call out at a California farmers market.

California's modern agricultural legacy began with progressive farmers who took advantage of the Gold Rush to turn the great expanses of fertile soil into much needed food. They were among the first farmers to turn to agricultural advances, such as intensive monoculture crop production. Today, we are paying the price, as over half of the organic matter in the soil has been lost since the dawn of California agriculture, and the state faces unprecedented challenges related to issues like water, urbanization, invasive species, and climate change. The good news is that California leads the nation with the highest number of farmers markets, as well as organic farms and sales. And the state's climate change legislation aims to reduce greenhouse gas emissions related to agriculture to pre-1990 levels.

This sunny mindset is on full display when you visit one of California's 764 farmers markets, which are operated in cities all across the state. One of my favorite pastimes is to make a stop at the local farmers market in whichever hamlet, whether big or small, I find myself in. The Santa Monica farmers market may be the most famous, with its cadre of LA chefs hand-selecting weekly produce for their menus. However, San Francisco's bustling Terminal Ferry Farmers Market provides you glimpses of exotic produce and hand-fermented pickles among an eclectic throng of socialites, techies, and activists. The Hollywood farmers market might be small, but the clients run from starlets to Goth rockers to rough bikers at this hotspot, which also happens to boast fabulous produce. Then there are those tiny farmers markets—maybe ten or so tables under tents—in nearly every town, where at least a couple of farmers will bring their seasonal goods: carrots, radishes, and greens in the winter; peas, fava beans, and asparagus in the spring; berries, peaches, melons, and tomatoes in the summer; squashes, persimmons, and apples in the fall.

Over the years, you get to know the farmers. You ask them their secret for growing tomatoes organically. How their harvest of sweet corn came in this summer. What the recent heat wave did to their crops. You see the farmers making their way from market to market—maybe Pasadena on Saturdays, Echo Park on Fridays. You fall in love with that particular variety of melons the farmer from Riverside grows, and look forward to next summer's harvest. You ask the olive grower at Pasadena when the next olive oil milling will occur, so he can set back some bottles for you. You find yourself looking forward to each season and letting that reflect in the foods you serve on your table. Scientists have found that when you shop at a farmers market, you eat more fruits and vegetables during the week, and you practice healthier behaviors. Of course, you do! Pack your fridge and pantry with farm-fresh produce each week, and reap the rewards in the joy of eating and optimal wellness.

Bringing the Farmers Market to Your Kitchen

No matter where you live, you can eat a rainbow of seasonal produce fresh from the farm.

· Learn about farmers markets and CSAs (community supported agriculture) in your neighborhood. Even if you live in a colder climate, seasonal produce is typically available in the summer months, which can reach into spring and fall.

· Grow some of your own food. The best farmers market can be in your backyard. Whether it's a tomato plant in the summer, or an herb pot on your balcony, grow at least some of your weekly produce.

· Honor special foods in your bioregion. California may be home to avocados and lemons, but they just can't beat Washington for apples and Virginia for peanuts. Discover the unique growing climates and produce in your own region and incorporate them into your culinary style.

Spring Pea Hummus

The first sweet, tender peas of the spring can't be beat. Sometimes farmers markets are the only place you can find these treasures, unless you grow the delicate tendrils and vines (which are edible, by the way) yourselves. They offer just the right verdant earthiness to this classic hummus recipe. Making your own home-made hummus is a cinch—just throw the ingredients into the blender or food processor and whiz them up to make a creamy, delicious hummus in no time. This is a go-to dip for veggies, a spread on sandwiches and wraps, an accompaniment for whole grain crackers or flatbread, a topping for salads, and a sauce for savory entrées, such as veggie balls, lentil patties, and falafels. So, go forth and be creative with your hummus!

SERVES 10

1 15-ounce can chickpeas, drained (reserve juice)

2 garlic cloves, minced

3 tablespoons lemon juice

2 tablespoons tahini

2 teaspoons extra-virgin olive oil

½ teaspoon red pepper flakes

1 cup fresh green peas, blanched, drained (or frozen peas, thawed, drained)

Salt (optional)

Place drained chickpeas, garlic cloves, lemon juice, tahini, olive oil, red pepper flakes, and peas in the container of a blender or food processor.

Process mixture until smooth, scraping down sides as needed. Add just enough reserved chickpea juice to make a smooth, thick hummus. Season with salt, as desired (optional).

Chill until serving time.

Serve with whole wheat pita, fresh veggies, and sandwiches.

Makes 2½ cups (about ¼ cup per serving).

Nutrition information per serving: 78 calories, 4 g protein, 10 g carbohydrates, 3 g fat, 1 g saturated fat, 3 g fiber, 3 g sugar, 184 g sodium

Mediterranean Tofu in Parchment

Showcase fresh summer tomatoes and herbs in this simple, straightforward, Mediterranean adaptation featuring protein-rich tofu. Heap up these wine-infused, caper and herb tomatoes over bricks of tofu, fold into a parchment bundle, and roast the whole affair until it's as rich and golden as the California sun. While this entrée looks utterly elegant, it's super simple; you can get it on the table in under thirty minutes.

SERVES 6

1½ tablespoons extra-virgin olive oil

3 cloves garlic, minced

1½ cups cherry tomatoes, cut in half

2 tablespoons fresh herbs, chopped (oregano, basil, thyme, tarragon, rosemary, sage, parsley)

2 tablespoons capers, rinsed, drained

2 tablespoons white wine

Freshly ground black pepper, as desired

Sea salt, as desired

1 15-ounce package tofu, extra firm, drained

6 10-inch rectangular pieces of unbleached parchment paper

Preheat oven to 400°F.

In a medium saucepan, heat olive oil. Add garlic and sauté for 2 minutes. Add cherry tomatoes, herbs, and capers and sauté for 2 minutes.

Add white wine and sauté for 2 minutes.

Slice tofu into six horizontal, rectangular strips.

Place each piece of tofu in the center of a piece of parchment paper.

Top each tofu with one-sixth (about 3 tablespoons) of the tomato-herb mixture.

Roll each parchment around the tofu by first bringing the sides of the parchment together, and then folding the seam along the length of the paper, then twisting each end similar to a candy wrapper.

Place each tofu parchment bundle on a baking sheet. Place the baking sheet on the top rack of the oven and bake for 10–15 minutes, until paper is golden brown and mixture is bubbly.

Serve the entire parchment paper bundle on each serving dish (or all on a large platter).

Nutrition information per serving: 113 calories, 7 g total fat, 1 g saturated fat, 89 mg sodium, 0 mg cholesterol, 4 g carbohydrates, 1.5 g fiber, 1 g sugar, 7.5 g protein

Roasted Butternut Squash Soup with Hazelnuts

Nearly every farmers market offers winter squash beginning in the late summer to early fall. These rich, golden-fleshed veggies originated in the Americas, and were an important part of the Three Sisters growing tradition. The Native Americans knew a thing or two, because squash, it turns out, is a powerhouse of nutrition, containing fiber, slow-digesting carbs, and carotenoids that promote heart health and reduce inflammation. And by roasting the squash before making a soup, you can maximize the sweet, earthy flavors of the squash and let them shine right through in the soup bowl. Just roast the squash in the oven or on a grill, sauté the veggies and herbs in a pot with broth, and then whiz it all up in a blender. Garnish with crunchy, nutty hazelnuts, fresh herbs, balsamic vinegar, and extra-virgin olive oil to make the soup really sing.

SERVES 8

For the squash:

1 medium butternut squash

1 tablespoon extra-virgin olive oil

Salt and black pepper (optional)

For the soup:

1 tablespoon extra-virgin olive oil

2 small yellow onions, diced (about 1½ cups)

1 cup diced celery

4 cloves garlic, minced

1 tablespoon ground sage

1 tablespoon ground thyme

4 cups vegetable broth

½ cup plant-based milk, plain, unsweetened (soy, almond, coconut)

1 tablespoon flour

Salt and black pepper (optional)

Preheat oven to 400°F (or heat grill, as an alternative method of roasting).

Split squash in half and scoop out seeds with a spoon. Slice each half into smaller pieces (about six per each half).

Place squash, peel facing down and flesh facing up, in a baking dish with ½ inch of water on the bottom; drizzle with 1 tablespoon olive oil and season with salt and black pepper (optional). Roast on top rack of oven for about 25 minutes, until tender when pierced with a fork. (Alternatively, grill seasoned squash on a hot grill until tender.)

While squash is roasting, heat 1 tablespoon olive oil in a heavy, large pot. Sauté onions, celery, and garlic for 8 minutes. Add sage, thyme, and vegetable broth and simmer for 10 minutes.

When squash is tender, spoon out flesh in chunks and place in the pot with soup mixture, stirring well while heating for 2 minutes.

Stir plant-based milk and flour together to make a roux. Stir into pot with soup mixture and cook until thickened (about 2–3 minutes).

Remove from heat and transfer to a blender in small batches (do not overfill blender to avoid spilling), processing until smooth and creamy.

For the garnish:

2 tablespoons chopped hazelnuts

Fresh sage, balsamic vinegar, and extra-virgin olive oil (optional)

Serve in individual soup bowls. Makes about 1 cup per serving.

Garnish with chopped hazelnuts, fresh sage, and a drizzle of balsamic vinegar and olive oil.

Nutrition information per serving: 262 calories, 10 g total fat, 1 g saturated fat, 0 mg cholesterol, 599 mg sodium, 45 g carbohydrates, 8 g fiber, 11 g sugar, 5 g protein

Smashed Avocado Toast with Candy Radishes

We've been spreading gobs of extra ripe avocado over our toast in California for years now. So, when this essential dish became a trend, we celebrated the avocado toast buzz as whole-heartedly as ever. The simple act of smashing ripe avocados in a dish, with a dusting of seasoning and a squirt of lemon juice to keep it bright, is the smartest thing to happen to sliced bread, since well, sliced bread! Skipping out on more processed toppings (think margarine, jam, mayo) in lieu of avocados—packed with healthful fats and phytochemicals—is a heart-healthy trick in your plant-based arsenal. And now that we've got smashed avocado toast done, the next step is to get creative with your toppings. The spicy-crisp bite of candy-colored radishes in shades of soft pink, fuchsia, purple, red, and white is the perfect balance to that creamy green avocado.

SERVES 4

For the smashed avocado:

1 large avocado, ripe

1 tablespoon lemon juice

1 clove garlic, minced

Salt and pepper as desired

For the toast and toppings:

4 slices rustic, whole grain bread, toasted

8 assorted pink, white, purple, and red radishes, trimmed, sliced thinly

Freshly ground black pepper, fresh chopped herbs (optional)

Prepare smashed avocados by slicing avocado in half, scooping out flesh, and placing it in a small bowl. Mix in lemon juice, minced garlic, and salt and pepper as desired.

Toast whole grain bread.

Divide smashed avocados among four toast slices (about 3 tablespoons each) and spread evenly over surface.

Arrange sliced radishes over toast slices. Garnish with freshly ground black pepper and fresh chopped herbs, if desired.

Serve immediately.

Nutritional information per serving: 153 calories, 9 g total fat, 1 g saturated fat, 118 mg sodium, 0 mg cholesterol, 16 g carbohydrates, 6 g fiber, 2 g sugar, 5 g protein

Savory Green Bean and Macadamia Cheese Tart

Fresh green beans can be grown locally in California farmers markets several months out of the year, making them a favorite vegetable to feature in dishes like this savory, crispy tart. Packed with fiber and protein, green beans are one of nature's rock stars, even enriching the soil as they fix nitrogen from the air to deposit into the earth. Look for vegan, whole wheat filo dough sheets in your natural foods market. Just brush olive oil between the layers, and then top with a house-crafted easy macadamia nut cheese, then sautéed greens beans. Bake and slice into squares to serve as an entrée for brunch, lunch, or dinner. Or slice into smaller appetizer servings for a starter course.

SERVES 8

For the macadamia nut cheese:

1½ cups macadamia nuts, raw

Water, as needed

1 garlic clove

7–9 tablespoons plant-based milk, plain, unsweetened

1 tablespoon lemon juice

2 tablespoons nutritional yeast

Pinch salt and white pepper

For the pastry:

10 sheets filo dough, whole wheat, vegan (⅔ of 1-pound package), thawed

¼ cup extra-virgin olive oil

To make the macadamia nut cheese: Place macadamia nuts in a bowl and cover with water. Soak for 1 hour. Drain nuts and place in a food processor or small blender. Add 5 tablespoons plant-based milk, lemon juice, nutritional yeast, salt and white pepper and process until smooth. May need to pause, scrape down sides, and add additional plant-based milk as needed to make a very thick, creamy mixture. Set aside.

To prepare the pastry: Line a baking sheet with parchment paper. Place one sheet of filo dough on the lined baking sheet. Place olive oil in a small dish. Brush the surface of the filo dough very lightly with olive oil, using a pastry brush. Lay the second sheet of filo dough on top of the first sheet, and brush lightly with olive oil. Repeat steps, ending with the tenth sheet of filo dough (no need to brush the top of this sheet with olive oil). Set aside.

To prepare the green bean filling: Heat 1 tablespoon olive oil in a large saucepan. Sauté onion, garlic, and green beans for 2 minutes. Add water and balsamic vinegar, and sauté for an additional 2 minutes. Add thyme and mushrooms, and sauté for 2 minutes more. Set aside.

For the green bean filling:

- 1 tablespoon extra-virgin olive oil
- 1 red onion, sliced thinly
- 1 clove garlic, minced
- 12 ounces small, fresh green beans, trimmed
- 2 tablespoons water
- 1 tablespoon balsamic vinegar
- 1 teaspoon thyme
- 4 ounces mushrooms, sliced

Preheat oven to 400°F.

To assemble the tart: Evenly dot macadamia nut cheese over filo dough. Arrange green bean mixture on top. Place in hot oven and bake about 20 minutes, until golden brown.

Remove from oven and slice with a pizza cutter into eight pieces.

Nutritional information per serving: 388 calories, 29 g total fat, 4 g saturated fat, 143 mg sodium, 0 mg cholesterol, 29 g carbohydrates, 6 g fiber, 3 g sugar, 8 g protein

7

Hollywood Hopes

Hollywood has long been a fan of living la vida plant-based, with scores of stars lining up to eschew eating animals. But in the last few years this trend has really taken off, with a long list of celebrities who eat plant-based for a variety of reasons: health, performance, environment, ethics, and animal welfare. In fact, the entire celebrity crew from the hit movie *Avengers Infinity War*, including Benedict Cumberbatch, Chadwick Boseman, Mark Ruffalo, and Chris Hemsworth, all went vegan to prepare for their physically rigorous roles. And the Golden Globes has even served a completely plant-based meal for the glitterati in attendance.

While it may seem that the plant-based trend is a new thing among the stars, it's actually been around for a very long time among the famous, glittering set of society. The ancient Greek philosopher and mathematician Pythagoras restricted meat in his diet for ethical beliefs. Leonardo da Vinci avoided eating animals because of his dismay over how they were raised and killed in the name of food. Mary Shelley, author of *Frankenstein* (in itself, a story highlighting the horrors of slaughterhouses), found the idea of eating animals incompatible with her ethics. Another famous author, Leo Tolstoy, rejected the idea of killing animals on the basis of morality. Even brainy Albert Einstein eschewed eating meat, famously

A painter's palette of eggplants, ranging in shades from white to lavender to purple to black, for sale at the Ojai Farmers Market.

saying, "Nothing will benefit human health and increase the chances for survival of life on earth as much as the evolution to a vegetarian diet." Those are basically the same words scientific reports, including from the UN's Food and Agriculture Organization and the EAT-Lancet Commission, are saying today, decades later, when it comes to solving the issues of feeding 10 billion people a healthy diet within our planetary boundaries. One of the most important things we can *all* do is to eat a mostly plant-based diet to save our natural resources, avoid deforestation, reduce global warming, and keep people fed and healthy.

Hollywood and its stars have an enduring soft spot for saving the planet. Just look at Leonardo DiCaprio's foundation, which has awarded $100 million in grants to fund projects aimed at preserving the long-term health of the Earth's inhabitants. A plant-based eater, he's also investing in vegan food brands and has executive-produced plant-based documentaries (such as Kip Andersen's *Cowspiracy*). And then there's the dedication that *Titanic* director James Cameron and his wife Suzy—she met James while making the film—have exhibited when it comes to their passion for the environment (on full display in his movie *Avatar*). The pair have been vegan since 2012, and are enthusiastically involved with numerous projects to promote plant-based eating and sustainability, including founding a California school based on practicing plant-based eating and sustainability. All it took was reading Jonathan Safran Foer's book *Eating Animals* (one I highly recommend) for the talented Natalie Portman to become vegan. She went on to narrate the documentary by the same name. Mayim Bialik, Alicia Silverstone, Paul McCartney, Zac Effron, Beyonce . . . the list of plant-based celebrities goes on and on.

And why does it really matter what movie stars choose to eat or not eat? Because all it takes is one word out of Beyonce's mouth, one interview with climate activist and vegan Greta Thunberg on Leonardo DiCaprio's Instagram, and one photo of Pamela Anderson in a bikini with the names of meat cuts stenciled on her body, to change the minds of multitudes.

Become a Star-Powered Influencer

You can positively influence the lives of those you love, as well as those in your community, by being a beacon of light (without being annoying!).

- Kindly request plant-based options in your favorite eateries, markets, and food service operations in your community. If there is a demand, it might just get filled!

- Be the one to bring plants. At every party, social gathering, or snack break, be the one to bring a delicious, plant-based dish, showcasing just how approachable and delicious it is to eat vegan.

- Be gorgeous you! Eat well, feel good, and glow. Bring that glow with you wherever you go, to shine the light on the health benefits of plant-based eating.

Flower Power Salad with Rose Vinaigrette

Edible flowers—marigolds, nasturtium, pansies, roses, and more—are pure glowing beauty atop a tender green salad. Look for edible flowers at farmers market, supermarkets, and even your own garden (as long as you don't use chemicals, or have dogs using the area for their outdoor restroom!). I find these lovely flower petals in my local farmers market each week, but I also keep a supply of seasonal flowers growing in my California garden year-round. Tossed with fresh berries, hemp seeds, shredded coconut, chia seeds, and a rose tea-infused dressing, this pretty salad is much more than meets the eye—it's packed with powerful nutrition, too. The berries (and flowers) offer powerful antioxidant compounds, plus the hemp and chia seeds are rich in heart-healthy omega-3 fatty acids.

SERVES 4

6 cups mixed baby salad greens

¼ cup edible flower petals (cornflower, sunflower, pansies, chrysanthemum, rose, lavender, nasturtium, calendula, and herb flowers)

1 cup fresh assorted berries (raspberries, blueberries, blackberries)

1 tablespoon hemp seeds

1 tablespoon chia seeds

1 tablespoon shredded coconut, unsweetened

5 tablespoons Rose Vinaigrette (page 111)

Place salad greens, flower petals, berries, hemp seeds, chia seeds, and coconut in a salad bowl.

Drizzle with Rose Vinaigrette and gently toss, just until well combined.

Serve immediately.

Makes about 1¾ cups per serving.

Nutrition information per serving: 123 calories, 9 g total fat, 2 g saturated fat, 0 mg cholesterol, 17 mg sodium, 10 g carbohydrates, 3 g fiber, 5 g sugar, 3 g protein

Rose Vinaigrette

Did you know you can make a lovely vinaigrette with concentrated teas? The aromatic, floral flavors and astringency complement extra-virgin olive oil oh so well, as in the case of this Rose Vinaigrette. This recipe calls upon rose herbal tea to create a strong tea concentrate in order to carry the flavor gently into your next salad.

SERVES 4

3 tablespoons boiling water

1 rose herbal tea bag

1½ tablespoons extra-virgin olive oil

½ teaspoon agave syrup

Freshly ground black pepper

Sea salt (optional)

Place boiling water in a small cup and add tea bag.

Allow to steep at room temperature for at least 30 minutes.

Remove tea bag and squeeze out liquid.

Mix cooled tea with olive oil, agave syrup, black pepper, and sea salt (optional) in a small dish until smooth.

Toss into salad as desired.

Nutrition information per serving: 47 calories, 5 g total fat, 1 g saturated fat, 0 mg cholesterol, 0 mg sodium, 1 g carbohydrates, 1 g sugar, 0 g fiber, 0 g protein

Super Acai Berry Power Bowl

Dark purple-blue acai, blueberries, and blackberries form the backbone of this super-nutritious power bowl, which offers a healthy dose of phytochemicals linked with reducing oxidative stress and inflammation. Together with gluten-free whole grain quinoa, this power bowl offers long-lasting nutrition—all for a light 232 calories in each satisfying serving. Mix up mason jar bowls to enjoy on-the-go for lunches, snacks, and post-workout refueling. Or simply enjoy this easy treat at home for a naturally sweet snack or dessert. Kids will love it too.

SERVES 2

1 3½-ounce package acai puree (frozen, thawed)

¾ cup cooked quinoa, chilled

1 tablespoon pure maple syrup

1 tablespoon chia seeds

½ cup blueberries

½ cup blackberries

2 tablespoons shredded, unsweetened coconut

Stir together acai puree, cooked quinoa, maple syrup, and chia seeds in a small bowl. Divide among two individual bowls.

Top each bowl with ¼ cup each blueberries and blackberries, and 1 tablespoon coconut.

Serve immediately.

Nutrition information per serving: 232 calories, 5 g total fat, 2 g saturated fat, 37 mg sodium, 43 g carbohydrates, 7 g fiber, 21 g sugar, 5 g protein

Detox Goji Berry Chamomile Granola

Concentrated chamomile tea flavors this hand-crafted granola recipe, which is packed with essential plant-powered ingredients, such as oats, hemp, almonds, walnuts, coconut, pumpkin seeds, sunflower seeds, tahini, goji berries, blueberries, and cocoa nibs. Those powerful ingredients ratchet up the nutrition value—and flavor—of this heart-healthy mix. It's pretty enough you can fill mason jars and share this granola as a gift, too.

SERVES 16

⅓ cup boiling water

2 chamomile tea bags

4 cups old-fashioned oats

¼ cup hemp seed

½ cup sliced almonds

½ cup walnuts, coarsely chopped

½ cup shredded, unsweetened coconut

¼ cup pumpkin seeds

¼ cup sunflower seeds

1 teaspoon ground cinnamon

⅓ cup tahini

2 tablespoons agave syrup

½ cup dried goji berries

½ cup dried blueberries, unsweetened

½ cup cocoa nibs, unsweetened

Pour boiling water into a small cup. Place two tea bags in the cup and allow to steep for 15 minutes, until it becomes very concentrated. Remove tea bags, squeeze out liquid, and set aside.

Preheat oven to 350°F.

In a large mixing bowl, combine oats, hemp seed, almonds, walnuts, coconut, pumpkin seeds, sunflower seeds, and cinnamon.

In a small pot, heat tahini, agave syrup, and reserved chamomile tea just until smooth and bubbly, mixing with a whisk (about 2–3 minutes).

Remove pot from heat and mix hot tahini mixture into the bowl with the granola mixture, stirring well to coat the dry ingredients.

Pour granola in a large baking sheet and spread evenly.

Place on top rack of oven and bake for about 20 minutes, stirring every 5 minutes, until golden brown.

Remove from oven and allow to cool. Mix in goji berries, blueberries, and cocoa nibs and stir well.

Store in an airtight container for up to 2 months.

Makes about 8 cups of granola (½ cup per serving).

Nutrition information per serving: 250 calories, 14 g total fat, 4 g saturated fat, 0 mg cholesterol, 32 mg sodium, 28 g carbohydrates, 6 g fiber, 6 g sugar, 8 g protein

Berry Bliss Energy Balls

Who needs packaged nutrition bars when you can make your own, hand-crafted energy balls, filled with whole plants? These minimally processed, naturally sweet treats can power your diet as a healthful snack, energy boost, or post-workout replenisher. You can whip up these no-bake balls in minutes in your food processor, then pack them away in a container in your freezer or fridge to grab all week long. At 110 calories each, these energy balls provide a boost of slow-digesting carbs, different types of fiber, healthy fats, protein, vitamins, minerals, and phytochemicals.

SERVES 24

½ cup oats

2 tablespoons hemp seeds

2 tablespoons chia seeds

2 tablespoons flaxseeds

¼ cup sunflower seeds

⅔ cup unsweetened
    applesauce

10 small dates, pitted

⅓ cup dried cranberries

½ cup dried blueberries

⅓ cup creamy peanut butter

1 teaspoon vanilla

⅓ cup unsweetened
    shredded coconut

Place oats, hemp seeds, chia seeds, flaxseeds, and sunflower seeds in the container of a food processor. Process for a few minutes, until ingredients are finely ground.

Add applesauce, dates, cranberries, blueberries, peanut butter, and vanilla and process until smooth. This may take a few minutes, as you may need to pause, scrape down the sides, and process again until mixture is smooth.

Pour mixture into a bowl, cover, and chill for about 1 hour.

Remove from refrigerator and form into small balls by hand. Place coconut on a dish and roll each ball into the coconut.

Store in an airtight container in the refrigerator or freezer until serving time.

Nutrition information per serving: 110 calories, 4 g total fat, 1 g saturated fat, 0 mg cholesterol, 2 mg sodium, 17 g carbohydrates, 3 g fiber, 11 g sugar, 3 g protein

Masala Chickpea Cauliflower Rice Bowl

The cauliflower rice trend is here to stay! Those tender grains of cauliflower resemble rice, but with a lighter touch of carbs and calories to boot. This ultra flavorful, vibrantly colored bowl packs on the nutrition and spice profile by way of hearty veggies, chickpeas, peanuts, and a masala sauce.

SERVES 4

For the masala sauce:

½ tablespoon vegetable oil

½ onion, diced

½ small green chili, finely diced

½ tablespoon grated fresh ginger

2 cloves garlic, minced

2 teaspoons ground cumin

1 teaspoon ground coriander

¼ teaspoon ground turmeric

¼ teaspoon black pepper

2 cups canned crushed tomatoes

2 tablespoons chopped fresh cilantro

1 teaspoon garam masala

1 tablespoon lemon juice

1 tablespoon brown sugar

Salt, as desired (optional)

To prepare the masala sauce: Heat oil in a skillet or sauté pan. Add onion, chili, ginger, garlic, cumin, coriander, turmeric, and black pepper, sautéing for 9 minutes, stirring frequently.

Add crushed tomatoes, cover with a lid, and cook for an additional 20 minutes, stirring occasionally.

Add fresh cilantro, garam masala, lemon juice, and brown sugar and mix well. Season with salt if desired.

Puree sauce until smooth with an immersion blender, or transfer to an electric blender or food processor to puree.

While masala sauce is cooking, assemble other bowl ingredients.

Heat cauliflower rice, according to package directions (if using fresh, simmer, sauté, or microwave until just tender, but firm).

Place peas in a microwave safe dish and heat 2 minutes, until warm, yet firm.

Place chickpeas in a microwave safe dish and heat 2 minutes, until warm.

Arrange four Masala Chickpea Cauliflower Rice Bowls as follows:

Fill each bowl (about 3-cup size) with one-fourth (about ¾ cup) of the warm cauliflower rice.

Top each bowl with one-fourth (¼ cup) of the warm peas.

Top each bowl with one-fourth (about ⅓ cup) of the warm chickpeas.

Top each bowl with one-fourth (½ cup) of the shaved red cabbage.

Top each bowl with one-fourth (½ cup) of the chopped cucumbers.

For the bowl ingredients:

1 pound (about 3 cups) fresh or frozen cauliflower rice (or finely chopped cauliflower)

1 cup frozen peas, defrosted

1 15-ounce can chickpeas, rinsed, drained

2 cups shaved red cabbage

2 cups chopped cucumber, with peel

⅓ cup peanuts

¼ cup chopped fresh cilantro

Top each bowl with one-fourth (about ½ cup) of the warm masala sauce.

Top each bowl with one-fourth (about 1½ tablespoons) of the peanuts.

Top each bowl with one-fourth (about 1 tablespoon) of the fresh cilantro.

Serve immediately.

Nutrition information per serving: 327 calories, 10 g total fat, 1 g saturated fat, 0 mg cholesterol, 481 mg sodium, 51 g carbohydrates, 12 g fiber, 11 g sugar, 14 g protein

Matcha Tea Nice Cream

The plant-based "nice cream" offerings have utterly exploded in recent years. But it's always fun to make a batch yourself to show off your culinary chops. This dainty yet rich plant-based ice cream is based on only five ingredients, with the star being matcha green tea—virtually brimming with anti-inflammatory compounds. Dust it with some dried rose petals and dark chocolate shavings to bring on the beauty.

SERVES 8

1 13.5-ounce can coconut milk (do not use coconut milk beverage or light coconut milk)

1 13.5-ounce can coconut cream

¼ cup agave syrup

1 teaspoon vanilla

1 tablespoon matcha green tea powder

For the garnish (optional):

Dairy-free dark chocolate shavings

Rose petals, dried

Combine coconut milk, coconut cream, agave syrup, and vanilla in a medium pan and heat over medium setting, stirring frequently, until mixture starts bubbling.

Remove from heat, add matcha tea powder, and mix with an immersion blender (or pour into a blender container) for 1–2 minutes, until very creamy and well combined.

Transfer mixture to a container, cover, and chill in the refrigerator until it completely cools down (about 2 hours).

Churn in an ice cream maker, following manufacturer's directions, until thick and creamy (depending on ice cream maker, about 5–15 minutes).

Place in a container in the freezer until it achieves desired firmness to scoop (about 1–2 hours).

Scoop into dishes and garnish with shaved dairy-free dark chocolate and dried rose petals, if desired.

Makes about 1 quart.

Nutrition information per serving: 283 calories, 27 g total fat, 24 g saturated fat, 0 mg cholesterol, 8 mg sodium, 13 g carbohydrates, 2 g fiber, 8 g sugar, 3 g protein

8

Ojai, Bohemian Paradise

Shangri-La. That's the official nick-name for Ojai, my new life place. Ojai is a small town nestled in a rich valley surrounded by mountains, located between Los Angeles and Santa Barbara. In fact, the name Ojai (pronounced *oh-hy*) is said to have originated from an indigenous term for the word *nest*. However, the name actually originates from the word *moon* in Chumash, the Native American tribe from this region. What's so special about Ojai, you ask? There are just so many reasons to fall

A glimpse from my home in Ojai, looking down at the family farm of The Ojai Vineyard's winemaker.

under its spell: The land, air, soil, mountains, people, and spirit of Ojai make one feel immediately at peace. Pilgrims have been coming here for centuries to study philosophy, art, Buddhism, and plant-based living.

If you looked up the area in a tour guide, you'd read that Ojai is a destination known for its boutique hotels, recreation opportunities, hiking, spiritual retreats, farmers markets, and local organic agriculture. And that pretty much sums it up. This place has been doing organics, farmers markets, sustainability, yoga, meditation, plant-based eating, art, theater, and caring for people, animals, and the planet long before it was a thing! This is fully on display in the mix of intriguing people who reside here, from farmers and environmentalists to spiritual leaders and movie stars... and everything in between. Just sit down at a café and you'll likely have an interesting conversation with someone within a few minutes. And while you're there, make sure you read the bulletin board, as you'll see so many things happening, from yoga retreats to marathons to regenerative agriculture meetups.

Ojai Valley flaunts its natural beauty, with its trickling streams and fields of golden mustard and meandering little flocks of quail and wild hare, all under the gaze of the majestic Topa Topa Mountains, which turn bright pink before sundown—known locally as "the pink moment." You'll spy charming citrus and avocado orchards, lavender and herb farms, and organic vegetable farms that spread like a colorful patchwork quilt over the valley. The availability of freshly harvested organic foods, in combination with a healthful, plant-based, new-age philosophy, unites to create a unique food scene. Food is casual here—on picnic tables with your dog at your feet—but it's *really good*, showcasing a farmer's fresh harvest for the day, along with an eclectic combination of cultural inspiration. And vegan options are simply a given. Case in point: Any night of the week you can dine in town on a macro wrap filled with grilled seitan, seaweed, and fermented vegetables with vegan miso mayo all wrapped up in a whole grain tortilla, complete with a namaste greeting.

Infuse your Kitchen with a California Boho Spirit

No matter where you live, you can invite some funky spirituality into your plant-based kitchen, with a few essential ingredients.

- Celebrate the pure, organic essence of plant foods in your eating style: aromatic citrus fruits, perfectly ripe avocados, a head of rugged kale, along with less-familiar veggies, such as turnips, celery root, and shishito peppers.

- Add a Bohemian flair to your cooking. Try fermented *everything* (kombucha, cauliflower, radishes, and carrots). Mix in some nutritional yeast for a touch of umami. And try old-school plant proteins made cool again, such as garbanzo paste, seitan, tempeh, and green lentils.

- Usher new-age, Eastern spirituality into your kitchen, by way of ingredients like sea vegetables, miso, and lotus root. Take a deep breath and savor the flavors.

Lavender Almond Cookies

This aromatic herb is used in many culinary applications, including savory dishes, salads, and desserts. While lavender grows well in many sunny regions of California, it can grow in cooler climates during the summer months. If you don't have a lavender plant to harvest the light purple flowers for your cooking pleasure, you can find the dried flowers at many cooking shops and online stores. This recipe features the trademark flavors of lavender in a delicate, tender almond cookie, capturing two trademark flavors of California. They are light and pretty enough for an elegant tea, yet delicious enough to appeal to even kids (both young and old!).

SERVES 20 COOKIES

- ½ cup aquafaba (see note on page 10)
- ¾ cup organic cane sugar
- ¾ cup softened dairy-free margarine
- 1 teaspoon pure vanilla extract
- ¾ cup almond flour or meal
- 1½ cups enriched, unbleached wheat flour
- 1 teaspoon baking powder
- ¼ teaspoon salt (optional)
- 2 tablespoons dried lavender flowers (see *Note*)
- ¼ cup finely chopped almonds

Preheat oven 350°F.

Whip aquafaba and sugar with an electric mixer until soft peaks form.

Gently fold in margarine and vanilla until smooth.

In a medium bowl, mix almond flour, wheat flour, baking powder, salt (optional), lavender flowers, and almonds together.

Gently fold dry ingredients into the aquafaba mixture, just until well distributed.

Spray two baking sheets with nonstick cooking spray. Drop batter by spoonfuls onto baking sheets.

Place in oven and bake for about 20–25 minutes, until firm and golden brown along edges.

Remove from oven and cool.

Note: Dried lavender flowers may be made at home by collecting, washing, and sun-drying lavender flowers, or you can purchase them at a well-stocked market or online shop. You can adjust the amount based on your preference. If you want a very mild lavender flavor, decrease amount to 1½ tablespoons. If you want a strong lavender flavor, increase to 2½ tablespoons.

Nutrition information per serving (1 cookie): 135 calories, 8 g total fat, 2 g saturated fat, 2 mg sodium, 7 mg cholesterol, 15 g carbohydrates, 1 g fiber, 8 g sugar, 1 g protein

Breakfast Tempeh Sweet Potato Salad

Yes, you really can have salad for breakfast! Especially if you call upon the hearty flavors of sweet potatoes, onions, and tempeh, mixed up with a savory blend of spices, herbs, and nutritional yeast, and tossed into a crisp salad featuring radishes and pumpkin seeds! Roast the veggies the night before to make this salad super simple the next day.

SERVES 4

For the roasted vegetables:

1 large sweet potato, peeled, cubed

1 small onion, sliced

8 ounce package tempeh, cubed

1 tablespoon extra-virgin olive oil

1 tablespoon balsamic vinegar

1 teaspoon cumin seeds

1 teaspoon smoked paprika

1 teaspoon oregano

2 tablespoons nutritional yeast

Salt, as desired

For the toast:

4 slices whole grain, rustic bread

For the salad:

1 head romaine lettuce, torn

1 bunch radishes, trimmed, sliced

2 small cucumbers, sliced

¼ cup pumpkin seeds

Extra-virgin olive oil and balsamic vinegar, as desired

Preheat oven to 400°F.

Place sweet potato cubes, onion slices, and tempeh cubes in a bowl and toss with 1 tablespoon extra-virgin olive oil, 1 tablespoon vinegar, cumin seeds, paprika, oregano, nutritional yeast, and salt (if desired).

Spread vegetables on a baking sheet and roast for about 25–30 minutes, until tender and golden. Remove from oven and cool slightly.

Place sliced bread on the racks of the hot oven while vegetables are baking, allowing to toast until golden brown (about 8 minutes).

Meanwhile, prepare salad ingredients by tossing together lettuce, radishes, cucumbers, and pumpkin seeds in a bowl. Toss in cooled sweet potato tempeh mixture.

Drizzle with olive oil and balsamic vinegar.

Divide into four large bowls and serve with one slice toasted rustic whole grain bread.

Note: This recipe may be prepped ahead of time by making the roasted vegetables in advance. It is also delicious for meal prep—prepare four salads and place them in airtight containers for use during the week (do not drizzle with oil or vinegar until immediately before eating).

Nutrition information per serving: 357 calories, 15 g total fat, 3 g saturated fat, 0 mg cholesterol, 145 mg sodium, 40 g carbohydrates, 9 g fiber, 9 g sugar, 22 g protein

Apple Fennel Slaw

Fennel, with its feathery leaves and licorice scent, is a common sight at the Ojai farmers market. Sweet-tart, crisp apples pair heavenly well with fennel in this cabbage-based slaw. Just a few ingredients tame these powerful flavors into a luscious, colorful slaw that is the perfect dish to serve at a picnic, outdoor barbecue, or potluck. The rugged textures of this slaw hold up for a few days, too, meaning you can pack it along for lunch the next day. I love this slaw piled up in a sandwich, such as my Barbecue Pulled Jackfruit Sandwich (page 206).

SERVES 8

For the salad:

1 fennel bulb

½ small head cabbage

2 carrots

½ cup raisins

For the creamy caraway dressing:

1 lemon, juiced

½ cup vegan mayonnaise

1 tablespoon Dijon mustard

1 teaspoon agave syrup

1 teaspoon caraway seeds

½ teaspoon black pepper

Salt (optional)

Trim the leaves and stems of fennel to reveal the bulb, reserving ¼ cup chopped fennel fronds. Place reserved fennel fronds in a large salad bowl.

Using a food processor or mandoline, shave fennel bulb and cabbage thinly and add to the large salad bowl.

Using a food processor or box grater, shred the carrots and add to the large salad bowl.

Add raisins and toss gently.

To make the creamy caraway dressing: In a small bowl, add lemon juice, vegan mayonnaise, Dijon mustard, agave syrup, caraway seeds, black pepper, and salt as desired, mixing until smooth.

Stir the dressing into the vegetable mixture, combining gently until well distributed. Chill until serving time.

Makes about 2 quarts (8 cups).

Nutrition information per serving: 109 calories, 5 g total fat, 0g saturated fat, 0 mg cholesterol, 172 mg sodium, 15 g carbohydrates, 3 g fiber, 9 g sugar, 2 g fiber, 2g protein

Blood Orange Hazelnut Kale Salad

Citrus farms have been a historic part of the landscape in Ojai Valley, with their rows of bright green shrubby trees boasting orbs of golden fruit basking in the gentle sun. This recipe highlights the beautiful blood orange, which is packed with anthocyanins that bestow the deep ruby-red shade to the fruit. So, enjoy the harvest of blood oranges when they are in season, pairing the zesty fruit with pungent kale leaves, toasted hazelnuts, and a simple cumin cilantro vinaigrette.

SERVES 8

For the cumin cilantro vinaigrette:

1½ tablespoons extra-virgin olive oil

2 tablespoons fresh lemon juice

1 small clove garlic, minced

½ teaspoon cumin

¼ teaspoon paprika

¼ cup fresh, chopped cilantro

For the salad:

1 bunch fresh kale, cleaned, trimmed, sliced

3 small blood oranges, peeled, sliced horizontally into circles, seeds removed

¼ cup toasted hazelnuts, coarsely chopped

To prepare the cumin cilantro vinaigrette: In a small bowl, mix together olive oil, lemon juice, garlic, cumin, paprika, and cilantro. Set aside.

To prepare the salad: Place kale in a large salad bowl. Pour vinaigrette over kale and massage into leaves with clean hands for 1–2 minutes.

Arrange blood orange slices over the kale.

Sprinkle with hazelnuts.

Serve immediately.

Nutrition information per serving: 77 calories, 5 g total fat, 1 g saturated fat, 0 mg cholesterol, 10 mg sodium, 8 g carbohydrates, 2 g fiber, 4 g sugar, 2 g protein

Lemon Shishito Peppers

During the warm days of summer, you might be lucky enough to spy a basket of small, bright green shishito peppers. These mildly spiced and sweet peppers are the ideal size for grilling. Just marinate them in this flavorful vinaigrette and grill them until they are browned and tender. Then keep popping them in your mouth! Shishitos grow really well in California's sunny climate, but you can also spy them at farmers markets and supermarkets across the country. When you see shishitos, you simply must take them home and grill (or oven roast) these mini peppers as a starter or side dish to your outdoor meal.

SERVES 4

1 pound fresh shishito
   peppers, whole

For the marinade:

1 lemon, juiced

1 tablespoon extra-virgin
   olive oil

3 cloves garlic, minced

½ teaspoon smoked paprika

½ cup fresh cilantro or
   parsley, coarsely chopped

Pinch sea salt (optional)

Place clean, whole shishito peppers in a large bowl (do not trim stems).

Mix together lemon juice, olive oil, garlic, smoked paprika, cilantro or parsley, and salt (if desired) in a small bowl.

Pour marinade over shishitos, stir well, cover, and refrigerate for 1–2 hours.

Heat grill and place shishito peppers on a grilling basket or grilling platter (the small peppers fall through the grill grates easily).

Grill for about 8 minutes, until browned on surface. Serve immediately.

Note: May also roast shishito peppers in a baking sheet on the top shelf of a hot oven (400°F) for about 10–15 minutes, until browned.

Nutrition information per serving: 70 calories, 4 g total fat, 1 g saturated fat, 0 mg cholesterol, 3 mg sodium, 9 g carbohydrates, 0 g fiber, 0 g sugar, 1 g protein

Harvest Vegetable Grain Bowl with Dukah

Rustic, wholesome grain bowls are de rigueur in health-minded restaurants. But you don't need to dine out to reap the benefits of a bowl filled with whole grains, roasted vegetables, and a flavorful topping! Here's proof: This super delicious, satisfying grain bowl starts with cooked whole grain barley, topped with a cornucopia of fall veggies roasted in mustard vinaigrette, including cauliflower, carrots, sweet potatoes, and brussels sprouts, and dusted with the home-made spice blend dukah. Now you're all set for a divine meal.

SERVES 4

For the grains:

1 cup barley, uncooked

2 cups vegetable broth

1¼ cups water

For the harvest vegetables:

½ head cauliflower, separated into florets

2 medium carrots, sliced

1 medium sweet potato, peeled, cubed

8 ounces brussels sprouts, sliced in half

1 small red onion, sliced

1 15-ounce can cannellini beans (white beans), rinsed, drained

For the mustard vinaigrette:

2 tablespoons extra-virgin olive oil

2 tablespoons red wine vinegar

1 teaspoon whole grain mustard

2 cloves garlic, minced

Salt and pepper, as desired (optional)

To make the grains: Place barley and broth together in a small pot, stir, cover, and cook until grains are tender (about 35–40 minutes). Fluff with a fork.

To make the harvest vegetables: Preheat oven to 400°F. Place vegetables—cauliflower, carrots, sweet potato, brussels sprouts, red onion, beans—in rows on a baking sheet.

Make the mustard vinaigrette in a small dish by whisking together olive oil, vinegar, mustard, garlic, and salt and pepper as desired.

Drizzle the vinaigrette over the vegetables. Toss each row of vegetables with tongs.

Place vegetables on top rack of oven and roast for about 45 minutes, until golden brown.

For the dukah:

¼ cup pistachio kernels

2 tablespoons sesame seeds

1 tablespoon cumin seeds

1 tablespoon fennel seeds

1 teaspoon black
   peppercorns

½ teaspoon sea salt
   (optional)

Prepare dukah by heating a small skillet over medium heat. Add pistachios, sesame seeds, cumin seeds, fennel seeds, black peppercorn, and sea salt (optional). Toast for 2–3 minutes, until mixture becomes aromatic, but do not burn or blacken. Remove from heat, cool slightly, and grind in a spice grinder or small blender just for a few seconds—should be coarsely ground. Makes about ½ cup.

To serve: Divide barley among four serving bowls, top with vegetables, and sprinkle with dukah (as desired). Serve immediately.

Nutrition information per serving: 529 calories, 15 g total fat, 2 g saturated fat, 0 mg cholesterol, 171 mg sodium, 86 g carbohydrates, 21 g fiber, 9 g sugar, 19 g protein

9

Heartland of California

The Central Valley of California is really something to behold. Running parallel to the Pacific Ocean, this vast, flat valley stretches approximately 60 miles wide and 450 miles long. Thanks to its deep history—the valley slumbered beneath a sea for millennia before the mountain ranges rose up to the east, shedding off sediments that enriched the valley—the Great Valley (as it is called) is one of the most fertile growing regions in the world. Bestowed with a Mediterranean climate, this part of California produces more than half of the nation's fruits, vegetables, and nuts.

And, oh, these are some of our most prized foods! It is here that farmers produce the bulk of our country's berries, tomatoes, nuts, artichokes,

A beautiful posey of an artichoke, captured among a field of artichokes in California.

grapes, apricots, olives, carrots, and asparagus. And that's not all. You will also find beans, grains (even rice!), citrus, greens, celery, kiwi, broccoli, melons, squash, and pomegranates, among many other crops. More than 230 crops are grown in the valley, and farmers take full advantage of the 300 days a year of sunshine to plant a quick-growing vegetable crop, then rotate it out for another crop after the harvest is over. These handy farmers are able to rapidly accommodate the latest fad, from kale to cauliflower, making sure there is a constant supply in your supermarket. This agricultural hub is the reason you can find fresh veggies in your supermarket in the wintertime. Skilled farm workers in California—the first state to pass overtime pay for farm laborers—hand harvest many of the tender vegetable crops, such as berries, artichokes, and kale.

A drive through the heartland of California may yield numerous agricultural views, from submerged rice fields with snow-white egrets prancing in the water to perky farms with globe artichokes, which look like overgrown thistles, bending in the breeze. While the vast growing region of California is typically home to large single-crop farms, you'll also find a growing number of organic farmers focusing on producing foods in a more biodiverse system, with more attention to the health of the soil, people, and planet.

It *really is* about eating locally here. Sacramento, the capital of California and at the valley's epicenter, is on a mission to be the farm-to-fork capital of the country. Indeed, my first encounter with farm-to-table eating—the very first time I observed a chef calling out the farm where the food was grown on the menu—was in this town. With access to such a bounty of regionally grown foods, you just can't help but eat from the farm every day. You can even check out seeds from the public library in Sacramento!

The spirit of the valley is all about pure foods prepared simply—it's about freshness and quality over fancy preparation style. It's about hearty eating to provide energy for the harvest.

Take to Heart a Simple, Locally Grown Food Style

Apply a lesson from the heartland by preparing simple, amazing foods that satisfy the spirit, soul, and body based upon seasonal, locally produced plants.

- Find favorite sources for local foods. Check out the foods that are available in your growing region, whether it's sweet corn or cucumbers, and pinpoint your favorite producers to ensure your farmer will have a revenue stream to keep supplying you with the best produce.

- Don't overly fuss with the flavors of really good produce. A drizzle of lemon juice and olive oil may be all those artichokes need when they are just that good.

- Keep it hearty! There's no need to feel weak-kneed at the end of the day on a plant-based diet. Include delicious foods that will fill you up until the next meal, such as chili, casseroles, and home-baked breads.

Creamy White Bean Chili

This light-colored chili is a pleasant take on a traditional tomato-based chili. Filled with white beans, hominy, green chilies, and herbs, it's comforting and satisfying all at once. This is the perfect party recipe—just let your guests fill up big steaming bowls, and serve it with cornbread and a crisp salad.

SERVES 12

1 1-pound bag small white beans, dried

4 cups vegetable broth

2 cups water

1 tablespoon extra-virgin olive oil

2 small white onions, diced

4 cloves garlic, minced

3 stalks celery, diced

1 yellow bell pepper, diced

2 teaspoons chili powder

2 teaspoons ground cumin

2 teaspoons ground oregano

1 4-ounce can diced green chilies, with liquid

1 25-ounce can white hominy, with liquid

2 limes, juiced

2 cups plant-based milk, plain, unsweetened

2 tablespoons flour

Garnish: chopped parsley, cilantro, or green onions

Place beans in a large pot, cover with water, cover with a lid, and soak overnight.

Drain soaking water from beans and add broth and 2 cups water.

Place on medium heat, bring to a simmer, and cook for 15 minutes.

Meanwhile, heat olive oil in a large skillet or saucepan over medium heat.

Add onions, garlic, celery, and bell pepper to olive oil. Sauté for 6 minutes.

Add chili powder, cumin, and oregano to vegetable mixture, and sauté for 2 minutes.

Add sautéed vegetable mixture to pot of beans, stirring well.

Add diced green chilies, hominy, and lime juice; stir well, cover, and simmer for an additional 60–70 minutes, stirring occasionally, until beans are tender yet retain their shape. Should have a thick, yet moist texture. If the mixture becomes too thick during the cooking process and starts to stick, add additional water as needed.

Whisk together plant-based milk and flour in a small dish. Add to pot and stir over medium heat, cooking until mixture is bubbling and thick (about 5 minutes).

Remove from heat and serve individually or in a large serving dish, garnished as desired with parsley, cilantro, and green onions.

Nutrition information per serving: 224 calories, 2 g total fat, 1 g saturated fat, 0 mg cholesterol, 239 mg sodium, 39 g carbohydrates, 13 g fiber, 4 g sugar, 11 g protein

Herb-Grilled Artichokes

Artichokes thrive in the agricultural heartland of California, emerging like giant flowers (they are actually in the thistle family) among the neat rows of silver-green foliage. Farmers simply crop off the flower on the stem when they are ripe, and these beauties make their way to you via farmers markets or supermarkets. You can grow this vegetable quite easily in warm climates in your backyard, too. Artichokes are best enjoyed simply: as fragrant, crispy grilled artichokes. These babies are rich in nutrients, too—fiber, as well as protein, vitamins C and K, folate, and phytochemicals.

SERVES 4

2 fresh artichokes

Herb marinade:

1½ tablespoons extra-virgin olive oil

1 lemon, juice and zest

2 cloves garlic, minced

1½ teaspoons Italian herb seasoning

Pinch black pepper and sea salt

Trim the top portion of the artichoke tops, and trim the stems.

Slice trimmed artichokes in half.

With a metal spoon, scoop out the blossom portion of the artichokes in the center.

Place artichoke halves in a medium pot with water and cook 10 minutes, until almost tender.

Place precooked artichokes in a baking dish.

To make the herb marinade: Whisk together olive oil, lemon juice and zest, garlic, Italian herb seasoning, salt, and pepper in a small dish.

Drizzle the vinaigrette over the artichokes and allow to marinate for about 30 minutes.

Grill the artichokes on a hot grill, first with cut side up and outside facing the heat for a few minutes, and then turn them over and grill for an additional 5 minutes, until golden brown.

Serve immediately.

Makes one-half artichoke per serving.

Nutrition information per serving: 84 calories, 5 g fat, 1 g saturated fat, 0 g cholesterol, 62 mg sodium, 9 g carbohydrates, 3 g fiber, 2 g sugar, 2 g protein

Confetti Avocado Veggie Dip

A creamy avocado dip is the start of so many good things. You can lighten it up by packing in a few extra veggies—along with their flavor, health, and crunch. California is one of the few climates in the world ideal for growing avocados. The year-long pleasant weather and good soils welcome the growth of this fruit, which is unique in the plant kingdom because of its abundance of healthful fats. The bushy, green trees are a truly regional sight, brightening the spirits, as well as the palate.

SERVES 6

1 large ripe avocado

1 clove garlic, minced

¼ cup chopped parsley

¼ cup sliced green onion

¼ cup chopped bell pepper (red, orange, or yellow)

¼ cup diced cucumber

5 small cherry tomatoes, cut in quarters

1 small lemon, juiced

Salt and pepper, as desired

Slice avocado in half, remove pit, and scoop out flesh into a medium bowl. Mash avocado with a fork until somewhat smooth.

Stir in garlic, parsley, green onion, bell pepper, cucumber, tomatoes, and lemon juice, combining until smooth. Season with salt and pepper as desired.

Serve immediately with tortilla chips, crackers, tacos, sandwiches, wraps, burritos, or fresh vegetables.

Makes about 2½ cups.

Nutrition information per serving: 59 calories, 5 g total fat, 1 g saturated fat, 0 mg cholesterol, 20 mg sodium, 4 g carbohydrates, 1 g sugar, 3 g fiber, 1 g protein

Orange Almond Olive Oil Cake

The heartland of California is truly a Mediterranean climate, as evidenced in all three of the major ingredients in this simple, light in sugar, yet moist and delicious cake: oranges, almonds, and olives. Set it out on a pretty plate and serve it in thick triangles to accompany tea or coffee.

SERVES 12

For the cake:

½ cup aquafaba (see note on page 10)

½ cup organic cane sugar

½ cup extra-virgin olive oil

1 large orange, juice and zest

1½ cups all-purpose wheat flour + 1 teaspoon, divided

1 teaspoon baking powder

⅓ cup finely ground almonds

For the topping:

2 tablespoons powdered sugar

1 large orange

Place aquafaba in the bowl of an electric stand mixer (or use a hand-held electric mixer) and add sugar. Whip until mixture is white and foamy and forms peaks. Set aside.

Preheat oven to 375°F.

Using a spatula, gently fold olive oil and the juice from one large orange into the aquafaba, just until moistened, being careful not to break the aquafaba texture.

Stir the zest from one large orange, 1½ cups flour, baking powder, and ground almonds together in a medium dish until well combined. Gently fold the flour mixture into the aquafaba mixture, just until dry ingredients are moistened and combined into mixture. Do not overwork mixture.

Spray a 9-inch round cake pan with nonstick cooking spray and sprinkle with 1 teaspoon flour. Shake flour in pan to coat it evenly, dumping out any excess flour. Gently spoon cake batter into the cake pan with a spatula, smoothing evenly.

Place cake pan in the center of the oven and bake for about 35–40 minutes, until golden brown and a fork inserted in center comes out clean.

Remove from oven and allow to cool for 2 minutes. Loosen edges with a knife and remove cake from pan, allowing it to cool for an additional 10 minutes on a rack.

Place cake on a serving dish. Sift powdered sugar over cake to dust it. Slice half of an orange into thin slices and arrange over the surface of the cake. With the remaining orange half, zest the peel and sprinkle orange zest over the top.

Slice into twelve wedges, and serve immediately.

Nutrition information per serving: 198 calories, 11 g total fat, 1 g saturated fat, 0 mg cholesterol, 1 mg sodium, 25 g carbohydrates, 1 g fiber, 12 g sugar, 2 g protein

Zucchini Walnut Biscuits

An abundance of summer squash in all sizes, colors, and shapes thrive in backyard gardens and small farms throughout California. One of the most popular is the zucchini. A single plant can bestow you with pounds of produce all year long, putting you in search of inventive ways to use this vegetable that just keeps on giving. Even if you don't have a zucchini plant, it's such a versatile veggie to toss in your farmers market bag and supermarket cart in the summer. Here's an intriguing way to showcase zucchini—in a tender, savory little biscuit, which can be served for breakfast or brunch, with a steaming bowl of soup or chowder for lunch or dinner, or as a treat with tea or coffee at snack time.

SERVES 12

- 2 cups enriched, unbleached wheat flour plus 1 tablespoon
- 1 cup whole wheat flour
- 1 cup finely chopped walnuts
- 2 tablespoons baking powder
- ½ teaspoon salt
- 1 teaspoon black pepper
- ½ cup unsalted vegan butter
- 1 cup plant-based milk, plain, unsweetened
- 2 cups shredded zucchini, drained well
- 2 cloves garlic, minced
- 2 tablespoons chopped chives

Preheat oven to 350°F.

In a mixing bowl, mix together 2 cups enriched, unbleached wheat flour and 1 cup whole wheat flour, walnuts, baking powder, salt, and black pepper.

Cut in pieces of vegan butter into the dry mixture with a fork until the mixture is crumbly.

Add plant-based milk and mix with a fork (or use clean hands) to make a smooth mixture—do not overwork dough.

Add zucchini (make sure to drain out any extra liquid), garlic, and chives and mix in with hands.

Sprinkle 1 tablespoon of enriched, unbleached wheat flour on a clean surface and roll out dough into a circle about 1-inch thick.

Using a 3-inch biscuit cutter (or the rim of a drinking glass), cut out circles in the dough to make twelve biscuits.

Spray a baking sheet with nonstick cooking spray and place the biscuits on the sheet.

Bake in oven for about 30 minutes, until golden brown and cooked through.

Nutrition information per serving: 269 calories, 16 g total fat, 4 g saturated fat, 113 mg sodium, 0 mg cholesterol, 28 g carbohydrates, 3 g fiber, 2 g sugar, 6 g protein

Fall Fruit and Wine Compote

Fall produce calls out for fruit-forward desserts, simply prepared based upon local foods. Honor the seasons with this simple, wine-soaked fruit compote, featuring pears, apples, dried fruits, citrus, and red wine.

SERVES 8

2 medium pears (red or green), unpeeled, cored, thinly sliced

2 medium apples (red, yellow, or green), unpeeled, cored, thinly sliced

½ cup dried prunes

½ cup dried cranberries

1 medium orange, zest and juice

2 tablespoons pure maple syrup

3 cups red wine

2 cinnamon sticks

½ cup hazelnuts, coarsely chopped

Place sliced pears and apples in a large pot. Add prunes, cranberries, the zest and juice of one orange, maple syrup, and red wine. Stir together to combine.

Add cinnamon sticks.

Cover and let stand for 1 hour.

Uncover the pot, place on medium heat, and simmer for about 15 minutes, until fruit is tender yet firm, and liquid is reduced and thickened, stirring occasionally.

Remove cinnamon sticks and dish warm compote into individual serving dishes or one large serving bowl.

Garnish with chopped hazelnuts.

Note: This compote is excellent served over plant-based vanilla ice cream.

Nutrition information per serving: 215 calories, 5 g total fat, 0 g saturated fat, 0 mg cholesterol, 4 mg sodium, 34 g carbohydrates, 4 g fiber, 23 g sugar, 2 g protein

California Ratatouille with Spaghetti Squash

I love using spaghetti squash as a plant-forward ingredient in salads, casseroles, and pasta dishes. It pairs so beautifully with my classic ratatouille recipe too. The sunny Mediterranean-California flavors of eggplant, zucchini, tomatoes, onions, olives, and capers warm up this recipe, which is absolutely packed with flavor, as well as nutrition power. A single serving of this recipe provides you with a rainbow of phytochemicals and antioxidant compounds. Just roast the squash in individual wedges, simmer up the ratatouille, and top each wedge of squash with a heaping serving of the ratatouille. This is simple enough to enjoy on a Wednesday night, yet pretty enough to serve for an elegant party.

SERVES 4

For the spaghetti squash:

1 small spaghetti squash

1 tablespoon extra-virgin olive oil

Salt and black pepper, as desired (optional)

For the ratatouille:

1 tablespoon extra-virgin olive oil

1 medium onion, diced

1 small eggplant, chopped

1 medium zucchini, chopped

2 cloves garlic, minced

1 14.5-ounce can diced tomatoes, with liquid

½ cup water

1 teaspoon basil

1 teaspoon oregano

1 teaspoon marjoram

¼ teaspoon black pepper

1 tablespoons capers, rinsed

½ cup Mediterranean olives, whole, drained

1 tablespoon balsamic vinegar

To prepare the spaghetti squash: Preheat oven to 400°F. Split the squash in half horizontally and scoop out the seeds. Cut each squash half into half again, to create four quarters.

Place spaghetti squash cut side up in a baking dish and add ½ inch water at the bottom of the dish. Drizzle with olive oil and season with salt and pepper, as desired (optional). Place on top rack of oven and roast until golden and tender (about 35–40 minutes).

To prepare the ratatouille: Heat olive oil in a large sauté pan or skillet. Sauté onions, eggplant, zucchini, and garlic for 10 minutes.

Add tomatoes, water, basil, oregano, marjoram, pepper, capers, olives, and vinegar. Cover and cook for 10 minutes, stirring occasionally, until vegetables are tender and mixture is thick.

When squash is done roasting, gently loosen strings of squash with a fork. Place squash on individual plates or a platter. Ladle ratatouille over squash.

Nutrition information per serving: 260 calories, 11 g total fat, 2 g saturated fat, 0 mg cholesterol, 543 mg sodium, 40 g carbohydrates, 10 g fiber, 19 g sugar, 6 g protein

10

Coastal California

One of my favorite travel recommendations for visitors to California is to take the scenic Route 1, which goes from north to south, running alongside the gorgeous Pacific coastline. It's our version of the Amalfi Coast in Italy or the Road to Hana in Hawaii. At almost 700 miles in length, the route offers glimpses of the Pacific marine ecosystem, coastline communities, and the diverse natural systems that exist on the shores. Driving from the south, you start in Orange County at Capistrano Beach, moving on to the artsy, tony enclave of Laguna Beach—a perfect crescent curve of sand and shore against the cliffs, with lovely homes

An unbelievably beautiful landscape, as a waterfall spills onto a beach with turquoise waves at Julia Pfeiffer Burns State Park in Big Sur.

lining the hills. Then on you go to the bustling beach towns of Los Angeles, such as Hermosa (now a Blue Zone Project community) and Venice, before heading to the more rural, agricultural Central Coast, with the picturesque city of Santa Barbara, replete with Spanish colonial homes topped with red-tiled roofs perched on the hills above the ocean, recalling some perfect Mediterranean village. Then come the majestic cliffs and redwood forests of Big Sur, followed by the rich history and unique sea life of Monterey, with its complex seafloor habitation and submarine canyons. And then finally on to the cultural mecca of San Francisco (the road takes you right over the Golden Gate Bridge), and the soft, curvy green hills of Marin and Mendocino.

California is determined to do its best to preserve the unique marine, marsh, and coastal ecosystems that are part of its rich natural tapestry. After all, the state has flora and fauna found nowhere else on the planet. Just take a look at its trees: California has the oldest known tree on Earth (the Methuselah pine), as well as 300-foot giant redwoods, and sequoias that stretch over 100 feet in diameter. Then there's the unique Monterey Bay, home to the nation's largest marine sanctuary, which is teeming with life, including kelp forests, deep sea canyons with animals adapted to darkness, and bright blue open seas filled with humpback whales, sea otters, elephant seals, and white sharks. And along these coasts, you'll find unique agricultural treasures too.

This mild—sometimes downright cold—climate means that numerous crops unsuited for the hot, dry Central Valley can be cultivated along the coast. Women seaweed farmers are harnessing the nutrition power of the oceans by harvesting local sea vegetables. Strawberry farmers take advantage of the cool coastal breezes and gentle rays of sunshine to harvest the most productive strawberry farms in the world. You can add other berries, such as blackberries and raspberries to that list. Tender lettuces also thrive in that moderate coastal climate, with 71% of the country's lettuce coming from the state. During the hot summer months, crops like carrots are farmed in cooler regions so that they can flourish. You can even forage wild plants in these parts, such as nettles, wild lettuce, sorrel, and mushrooms.

Remember, plant-based eating is closely aligned with preserving our beautiful planet and ecosystems. So, go ahead and let the gentle, quiet flavors of the coast inspire a whole array of plant-based dishes in your kitchen that honors our beautiful diverse and wild ecocystems. Pretty fresh berry salads, piles of sautéed mushrooms on toast, and unique greens in salads—even used for grilling.

Let Your Food Shine with a Gentle Spirit

Be thoughtful with your food purchasing, doing a little bit of homework about how the company sources its ingredients, as well as how it cares for the ecosystem.

- Avoid plastic as much as possible. It's estimated that by 2050 we will have more plastic in the ocean than sea life. Bring your own containers and shopping bags to reduce the amount of plastic you use.

- Try foraging. Learn about wild grasses, greens, and herbs in your region—with help from an expert or guide.

- Include more local berries. These gems are special, antioxidant-rich gifts from Mother Earth, and almost every region has its own varieties available in the summer.

Seaweed Soba Noodle Salad

Along the majestic coasts of California you'll find all manner of sea vegetables ready for harvesting. While these foods are treasured in cultures such as Japan, we have a ways to go in the US when it comes to including nutrient-rich sea veggies in our diets. However, it's exciting to see a growing appreciation for this plant food from the sea, in particular among local harvesters of wild seaweed along the coasts of Mendocino and San Francisco. Turn to seaweed to provide an umami, sea-like flavor to a variety of foods, including this soba noodle salad.

SERVES 8

For the salad:

1 ounce dried shitake mushrooms

1 cup boiling water

1 package (about 8 ounces) soba noodles

3 small Persian cucumbers, thinly sliced into matchstick strips

1 bell pepper (yellow, red, or green), thinly sliced

1 8-ounce package seitan, drained, chopped

½ cup dried, sliced seaweed (kelp, nori)

For the soy dressing:

1 tablespoon sesame oil

3 tablespoons soy sauce

½ tablespoon rice vinegar

1 teaspoon brown sugar

½ teaspoon wasabi paste

¼ teaspoon red pepper flakes

1 teaspoon minced ginger

1 clove garlic, minced

1 tablespoon sesame seeds

Place dried shitake mushrooms in a bowl and pour boiling water over them. Set aside for 20 minutes. Drain water. Slice thinly.

Fill a medium pot with water and bring to a boil. Place soba noodles in the pot and boil (according to package directions) about 4 minutes. Do not overcook. Place in a strainer and rinse well with cold water.

In a large bowl, mix together sliced cucumbers, sliced bell pepper, chopped seitan, sliced seaweed, cooked and cooled soba noodles, and sliced shitake mushrooms.

In a small dish, whisk together the sesame oil, soy sauce, rice vinegar, sugar, wasabi paste, red pepper flakes, ginger, and garlic.

Pour dressing over noodle mixture and toss well.

Place in a salad bowl or platter and garnish with sesame seeds. Chill until serving time.

Nutrition information per serving: 200 calories, 3 g total fat, 0 g saturated fat, 579 mg sodium, 34 g carbohydrates, 1 g fiber, 3 g sugar, 14 g protein

Roasted Chicory with Pistachios and Pomegranates

There are many types of edible chicories you can enjoy—they are easy to grow in your garden, too. These greens are closely related to lettuces, but with a bit more bitter, hearty taste. In fact, Belgian endives, escarole, and radicchio are in this family. While you can certainly tear these veggies into a fresh salad, you can also roast or grill them! They stand up quite well to a quick browning, which also can tame those bitter flavors.

SERVES 8

8 small heads chicory, trimmed, split in half lengthwise

1½ tablespoons extra-virgin olive oil

Freshly ground black pepper and sea salt, to taste

1 teaspoon chopped fresh rosemary (or ½ teaspoon dried)

1 tablespoon balsamic vinegar

¼ cup roasted pistachios

¼ cup pomegranate arils (seeds)

Preheat oven to 400°F.

Place chicory halves on a baking sheet, cut side facing up.

Drizzle with extra-virgin olive oil.

Sprinkle with black pepper and salt (to taste) and rosemary.

Toss with tongs to distribute ingredients well.

Place on top rack of oven and roast for about 10–15 minutes, until golden brown but still firm.

Remove from oven. Drizzle with balsamic vinegar, and sprinkle with pistachios and pomegranate arils. Serve immediately.

Nutrition information per serving: 58 calories, 5 g total fat, 1 g saturated fat, 3 mg sodium, 4 g carbohydrates, 2 g fiber, 1 g sugar, 1 g protein

Strawberry Salad with Brazil Nuts and Berry Vinaigrette

The cool coastal environs of California, stretching from Orange County in the south through Oxnard in Ventura County all the way up to Monterey in the north, is one of the most perfectly situated places on the planet to grow sweet, sweet strawberries! Tender butter lettuce is the backdrop for this fruity salad, which offers yet another way to highlight luscious strawberries—rich in sweet flavor and antioxidants—during their spring through summer harvest. This colorful salad is pretty enough for a buffet or holiday meal, yet it can also grace your lunch box or dinner table just as easily.

SERVES 4

4 cups tender lettuce greens, such as butter or mache

1½ cups sliced fresh strawberries

¼ medium red onion, sliced

¼ cup Berry Vinaigrette (page 167)

3 tablespoons chopped Brazil nuts

Freshly ground black pepper

In a large salad bowl, add lettuce, fresh strawberries, and red onion.

Prepare ¼ cup Berry Vinaigrette.

Drizzle the Berry Vinaigrette over the salad and toss gently. Sprinkle with Brazil nuts and freshly ground black pepper, and serve immediately.

Nutrition information per serving: 94 calories, 7 g total fat, 1 g saturated fat, 0 mg cholesterol, 27 mg sodium, 7 g carbohydrates, 2 g fiber, 4 g sugar, 1 g protein

Berry Vinaigrette

Create a truly flavorful dressing that captures the heart of freshly harvested, vine-ripened strawberries with this simple vinaigrette. It's perfectly suited to a simple green salad, and adds depth and layers to the Strawberry Salad with Brazil Nuts on page 164. It's also a delicious highlight in pasta or grain salads, or as a marinade for grilled vegetables or tofu.

SERVES 4

3 large, ripe strawberries

½ tablespoon extra-virgin olive oil

1 tablespoon sherry or champagne vinegar

¼ teaspoon black pepper

Pinch salt

Using a mortar and pestle, mash strawberries until fairly smooth. Stir in olive oil, sherry or champagne vinegar, black pepper, and salt with a fork.

Serve immediately with a salad, grain or pasta salad, or as a marinade for grilling.

Makes about ¼ cup vinaigrette.

Nutrition information per serving: 50 calories, 5 g total fat, 1 g saturated fat, 0 mg cholesterol, 25 mg sodium, 1 g carbohydrates, 0 g fiber, 1 g sugar, 0 g protein

Carrot Zucchini Spice Muffins

Carrots—which grow year-round in California—are an essential element in a plant-powered kitchen. With a long shelf life, they are so versatile in many dishes. Can you imagine a stir-fry, slaw, or smoothie without a cheerful, sunny carrot tossed in? These bright roots are also great in baked recipes, offering a burst of nutrition, color, and crunchy, sweet taste. This vegan version of a classic carrot spice muffin is a bit more healthful, with just a light touch of sweetness and the addition of whole grains, zucchini, nut meal, and hemp seeds.

YIELDS 9 MUFFINS

½ cup aquafaba (see note on page 10)

3 tablespoons coconut palm sugar (or brown sugar)

3 tablespoons coconut oil, melted

1 medium carrot (purple, orange, or yellow), shredded

1 small zucchini, shredded

½ cup plant-based milk, plain, unsweetened

1½ cups whole wheat flour

¼ cup nut meal (peanut, almond, or hazelnut)

3 tablespoons hemp seeds

1½ teaspoons baking powder

1½ teaspoons pumpkin pie spice

Pinch salt (optional)

¼ cup raisins

Preheat oven to 375°F.

Place aquafaba and coconut palm or brown sugar in the bowl of an electric mixer and whip for about 3 minutes, until fluffy.

Gently stir in by hand coconut oil, carrot, and zucchini.

Gently stir in plant-based milk.

Gently mix in whole wheat flour, nut meal, hemp seeds, baking powder, pumpkin pie spice, and salt (optional) until smooth.

Stir in raisins.

Spray a muffin pan with nonstick cooking spray or line with muffin papers.

Pour batter into muffin cups to fill.

Place in oven and bake until cooked through (about 50 minutes, makes a dense, moist muffin).

Remove from oven, cool slightly, and remove from pans.

Nutrition information per serving: 166 calories, 7 g total fat, 4 g saturated fat, 14 mg sodium, 23 g carbohydrates, 4 g fiber, 5 g sugar, 5 g protein

Sautéed Forest Mushrooms on Toast

In the cool, moist climate of Northern California, one can embark on a mushroom hunting adventure. Among the majestic redwoods, you can spy all manner of edibles, including perky mushrooms growing on the floor of the forest. Even if you don't go mushroom foraging in the wild, plenty of local farmers cultivate a variety of flavorful mushrooms, including hen of the woods, enoki, shitake, maitake, and chanterelles. I buy a big bag of mixed mushrooms from my local mushroom grower each week. They provide a miracle of meaty, umami flavors to plant-based dishes. This recipe is inspired by the simple dish in Sweden—after your basket is filled with mushrooms from the forest, you simple sauté a mountain load of them in the skillet and mound them over a piece of toast. That's it. My version has a bit of white wine (hey, it's California!) and thyme.

SERVES 2

4 ounces fresh mushrooms (crimini, maitake, shitake, chanterelles, oyster, hen of the wood)

1 tablespoon extra-virgin olive oil

1 teaspoon fresh or dried thyme

2 tablespoons white wine

Pinch sea salt

Freshly ground black pepper

2 slices rustic whole grain bread, toasted

Wash and coarsely slice mushrooms.

Heat oil in a small skillet.

Place mushrooms and thyme in skillet and sauté for 2 minutes.

Add wine and sauté for 6 minutes, until tender yet firm.

Season with salt and pepper as desired.

Pile half of the sautéed mushrooms on each toast to make an open-face sandwich. Serve immediately.

Nutrition information per serving: 144 calories, 8 g total fat, 1 g saturated fat, 0 mg cholesterol, 161 mg sodium, 14 g carbohydrates, 2 g fiber, 3 g sugar, 5 g protein

11

Inspirations from Asia

Waves of immigrants from Asia—China, Cambodia, Vietnam, Korea, Philippines, Japan, and beyond—have long made their way to California to follow their dreams, many as farmers. Approximately 75% of California's farm workers were Chinese in 1890. They came to California looking for a better life during the Gold Rush, many via small farms. Just about every mining camp hosted a Chinese farmer who grew vegetables to feed hungry souls searching for gold. The Chinese immigrants helped build the first transcontinental railroad, connecting the newfound California produce market stream to the rest of the country. These workers also made a huge contribution on the reclamation project for the Sacramento River Delta, which transformed the Central Valley into the bountiful farmland it is today. The Chinese farmers brought their advanced agricultural knowledge to their new homeland in California, as they helped develop systems for irrigation, crop rotation, and soil fertility. Sadly, despite all of their ingenuity, it didn't help these hard-working visionaries due to California's Alien Land Act, which restricted Chinese from owning land. This law wasn't declared unconstitutional until 1952.

A sassy sunset reflects on the waters in beautiful Goleta in Santa Barbara County.

Japanese immigrants also made a huge contribution to California agriculture before World War II, where they worked hard to transition from farm laborer to tenant farmer. By 1941, Japanese farmers were producing about 49% of the vegetables in California, in addition to helping to develop a distribution system for produce. Sadly, their role in agriculture was virtually obliterated during World War II, when 120,000 people of Japanese ancestry, mostly American citizens and farmers, were rounded up and incarcerated in internment camps, such as Manzanar in Inyo County, California. With lost homes and farms, even after the war was over many Japanese-Americans left farming forever.

Over 100,000 Filipinos came to the states during the 1920 and 1930s, many to farms as laborers. Through the decades, refugees from Cambodia, Laos, Vietnam, and Burma came to California to escape untold hardship, turning to farming in order to provide food for their communities. Many Asian-American farm workers suffered discrimination and exploitation, and in the 1960s they worked with Mexican-American farm workers to bring about positive change to farm worker rights.

When you think of the best in cuisines of Asia, your mind immediately travels to the beautiful color, crunch, and flavor of fresh vegetables. Vegetables are *everything* in these food traditions, from oyster mushrooms in a traditional sauce to bright greens sautéed with garlic to Thai basil and red chili peppers topping a curry. You can link Asian-Americans' dedication to high-quality, fresh produce in their culinary traditions directly to the farm-fresh abundance of vegetables in California's own eating aesthetic. Some of our most renowned chefs, including Alice Waters, have enlisted Asian-American farmers to supply them with the best of the best produce.

While California has become known for its bounty of salad greens, avocados, citrus, asparagus, and tomatoes, other more unusual Asian vegetables have been cultivated here for decades too. Tatsoi, long beans, daikon, lemongrass, okra leaf, Japanese pumpkins, and holy basil are just a handful of the crops that are grown in the Golden State. I can find a variety of these ingredients at my farmers market, where third-generation farm families produce a range of unusual vegetables that spark unique colors, textures, and flavors in my culinary style. You can also find a whole new world awaiting you in numerous Asian supermarkets and authentic eateries. Vegetarian traditions have always been common in Asian-American culture, with its Buddhist and Shinto religious roots promoting abstinence from animal flesh. Asia is where three classic plant proteins originate: the coagulated soymilk block we know as tofu, fermented grain and soy cakes called tempeh, and the wheat protein named seitan.

All of these amazing plant-based farming and eating traditions have made a huge mark on culinary eating traditions in the melting pot that is California. One of the best ways to enjoy plant-based foods is to take a dip into the flavorful cuisines of Asia.

Get to Really Know Cuisines of Asia

Authentic fare from many countries in Asia is becoming more available in towns across America. Try a few tips to make the most of this plant-forward eating style.

- Stir-fry vegetables more often. Mastering the simple art of cooking fresh vegetables in a very hot wok or skillet with a small amount of vegetable oil (peanut, sesame, soy), garlic, ginger, and soy sauce until crisp tender will change your life.

- Turn to soy sauce. This fermented soy brine is the "ketchup" of Asian cuisine, providing a rich umami quality and touch of saltiness to sauces, stir-fries, and curries.

- Try some unfamiliar vegetables. The next time you see an interesting vegetable, such as trumpet mushrooms, bok choy, or taro root, bring it home and give it a try. It will open up your palate to a whole new world of plant-based discovery.

Bitter Melon Seitan Stir-Fry with Brown Rice

California has a long history of Asian farmers tilling the earth, cultivating food to nourish the bustling region. They also brought with them traditional crops and foods of Asia, such as bitter melon, which grows well under the California sun. Bitter melon is a vegetable in the gourd family, which indeed is, well, bitter! Those properties in the vegetable actually have glucose-lowering benefits. A few tricks can help tame the bitterness of the vegetable, which I feature in this traditional Chinese-style stir-fry with seitan—a wheat-based protein with a long appreciation in China.

SERVES 4

1 bitter melon

1 tablespoon sesame oil

1 small onion, sliced

2 carrots, sliced

2 cloves garlic, minced

1 teaspoon minced ginger

1 bell pepper, sliced

8 ounces mushrooms, sliced

1 8-ounce package seitan, plain, chopped

3 tablespoons reduced sodium soy sauce

1 tablespoon agave syrup

1 tablespoon rice wine vinegar

1 teaspoon sriracha sauce (may adjust per spice preference)

3 tablespoons water

1 tablespoon cornstarch

1 tablespoon toasted sesame seeds

2 cups cooked brown rice

Slice bitter melon in half horizontally, scoop out seeds, and slice into thin slices.

Bring a small pot of water to boil, place sliced bitter melon in water, cover, and boil for 1 minute. Drain and place melon in ice water bath until cool.

Heat sesame oil in a large skillet or wok and add onions, carrots, garlic, ginger, and bell pepper, sautéing for 6 minutes.

Add mushrooms and sauté for 2 minutes.

Add cooked bitter melon and seitan, and sauté for an additional 2 minutes, until heated through and vegetables are crisp tender.

While vegetables are cooking, prepare the sauce by combining soy sauce, agave syrup, rice wine vinegar, sriracha sauce, water, and cornstarch in a small bowl, mixing until smooth.

Pour into skillet and stir-fry until sauce is thickened, about 1–2 minutes.

Sprinkle with sesame seeds.

Serve over cooked brown rice.

Nutrition information per serving: 448 calories, 7 g total fat, 1 g saturated fat, 472 mg sodium, 0 mg cholesterol, 49 g carbohydrates, 6 g fiber, 7 g sugar, 48 g protein

Snow Pea Udon Salad with Sesame Vinaigrette

The tender wheat-based Japanese udon noodle is fabulous in chilled salads, such as this super easy recipe, which can be prepared in under twenty minutes. It's all about the delicious sesame vinaigrette, which includes classic flavors of rice vinegar, soy sauce, ginger, garlic, peanuts, and sesame. Tossed with crunchy snow peas and carrots, this flavorful salad is the perfect addition to a meal, and can easily be toted along to a picnic, potluck, or work lunch.

SERVES 6

For the sesame vinaigrette:

1 tablespoon rice vinegar

2 tablespoons orange juice

3 tablespoons soy sauce

1 tablespoon sesame oil

2 tablespoons creamy peanut butter

½ teaspoon minced fresh ginger

2 medium garlic cloves, minced

¼ teaspoon crushed red pepper

1 tablespoon sesame seeds

For the salad:

1 9.5-ounce package dried udon noodles

8 ounces fresh snow peas, sliced in half

1 large carrot, thinly sliced

2 green onions, sliced

To make the sesame vinaigrette: Whisk together the vinegar, orange juice, soy sauce, sesame oil, peanut butter, ginger, garlic, crushed red pepper, and sesame seeds in a small bowl until smooth. Set aside.

To make the salad: Bring a medium pot of water to boil, add the noodles, and cook (according to package directions) for about 10 minutes, until tender but not overcooked. Rinse with cold water and drain.

Mix together the cooked noodles, snow peas, carrots, green onions, and vinaigrette until well combined. Serve immediately or chill until serving time.

Nutrition information per serving: 230 calories, 5 g total fat, 1 g saturated fat, 315 mg sodium, 40 g carbohydrates, 3 g fiber, 7 g sugar, 9 g protein

Vegetable Bibimbap Skillet

If you've never tried bibimbap, a Korean dish that means "mixed rice," now is your chance. I created this really easy version based upon this traditional dish, which is typically served in individual hot bowls, with crispy rice on the bottom, beautifully arranged vegetables on top, and a savory, spicy sauce over it all. You simply mix it all up at the table. This simplified version is created in one skillet, meaning less fuss and cleanup later on. It stars the Korean chili paste gochujang, tofu, carrots, zucchini, bell pepper, and greens.

SERVES 4

For the rice:

3 cups cooked short or medium grain brown rice (according to package directions)

For the marinade:

2 tablespoons sesame oil

2 tablespoons rice vinegar

2 tablespoons gochujang (Korean chili paste, look for vegan)

For the tofu:

1 15-ounce package firm tofu, chopped into 2-inch pieces

For the roasted vegetables:

2 medium carrots, sliced into matchstick pieces

2 small zucchinis, sliced into matchstick pieces

1 large bell pepper, sliced into matchstick pieces

2 garlic cloves, minced

Salt (optional)

Cook brown rice according to package directions and set aside.

While rice is cooking, prepare the remaining steps of the recipe:

Make the marinade by whisking together 2 tablespoons sesame oil with the rice vinegar and gochujang in a small dish.

Place the tofu in a microwave safe dish and pour half of the marinade over the tofu and marinate for 10 minutes, reserving remaining marinade. Heat the marinated tofu in the microwave for 4 minutes. Do not drain liquid.

To roast the vegetables: Preheat oven to 400°F. Place carrots, zucchini, and pepper on a baking sheet (sprayed with nonstick cooking spray) in a thin layer, sprinkle with garlic and salt (if desired), and roast on the top shelf of the oven until crisp tender, about 6–8 minutes.

To cook the greens: Place chopped greens in a medium pan with boiling water and steam just until tender, about 2 minutes. Drain any remaining water.

To assemble the dish: Heat a large skillet until very hot. Brush the bottom and sides of the skillet with 1 tablespoon sesame oil. Press cooked rice into the bottom of the skillet evenly, using a spoon. Place the skillet back on medium heat, cover, and cook for about 7 minutes, until the rice begins to get golden around the sides (do not stir).

For the cooked greens:

1 bunch greens (chard, bok choy, spinach), coarsely chopped

¼ cup boiling water

For the skillet:

1 tablespoon sesame oil

1 tablespoon sesame seeds

Remove the lid from the skillet and arrange hot greens, vegetables, and tofu over the rice. Drizzle remaining reserved marinade over the top and sprinkle with sesame seeds. Serve immediately right out of the skillet into bowls.

Nutrition information per serving: 377 calories, 15 g total fat, 2 g saturated fat, 159 mg sodium, 46 carbohydrates, 6 g fiber, 6 g sugar, 14 g protein

Yellow Curry with Tofu and Vegetables

I learned to make this authentic curry in Thailand, and went back home to search out the ingredients in California to re-create it. Plant-based dishes really shine in Southeast Asia, which produces a rainbow of abundant colorful produce just screaming to be highlighted in regional dishes. It's all about the home-made curry paste—every cook has his or her own secret combination of spices and herbs to create their favorite curry. You can find many of these ingredients in a well-stocked supermarket, and definitely at an Asian market or online.

SERVES 4

For the yellow curry paste:

4 red dried bird's eye (also called Thai) chili peppers

½ teaspoon roasted cumin seeds

½ teaspoon roasted coriander seeds

2 tablespoons chopped lemongrass (optional)

2 tablespoons chopped shallots

4 cloves garlic, chopped

1 tablespoon chopped fresh turmeric

1 teaspoon curry powder

For the vegetables and tofu:

4 small new potatoes, chopped

2 medium carrots, chopped

1 15-ounce can light coconut milk

2 bell peppers, sliced

1 15-ounce package extra firm tofu, cubed

¼ cup water

3 tablespoons soy sauce

1 teaspoon brown sugar

For the toppings:

10 leaves Thai basil

4 kaffir lime leaves (may used dried, optional)

1 fresh red chili pepper, sliced

Soak chili peppers in water for about 20 minutes, drain, and then chop.

Toast cumin seeds and coriander seeds in a small skillet for 1–2 minutes, just until warm (be careful not to burn).

Place the chili peppers, lemongrass, cumin and coriander seeds, shallots, garlic, fresh turmeric, and curry powder into a large mortar. Pound the ingredients with the pestle until the curry is ground thoroughly and resembles a paste.

Bring a medium pot of water to boil and add potatoes and carrots, cooking for about 8 minutes, until barely tender. Remove from heat, drain the water, and remove the vegetables.

Pour ¼ cup of the coconut milk into the saucepan. Add the curry paste and heat over medium, stirring well until it is fragrant and well combined (about 2 minutes). Add the cooked potatoes and carrots, bell peppers, tofu, the rest of the coconut milk, and water, and stir to combine, cover, and cook for 3 minutes. Add soy sauce and sugar. Combine well and cook just until bubbly and bell peppers are crisp tender (about 5 minutes).

Top with Thai basil, kaffir lime leaves, and red chili slices. Serve with brown rice.

Nutrition information per serving: 441 calories, 20 g fat, 7 g saturated fat, 335 mg sodium, 52 g carbohydrates, 9 g fiber, 6 g sugar, 23 g protein

Coconut Curry Corn Chowder

Classic Thai flavors of peppers, coconut, cilantro, lime, and curry are redolent in this super simplified soup. You can find all of the ingredients for this recipe in your local market, plus you can whip it up in under thirty minutes. This curried soup can serve as the focal point of a healthful plant-based meal—pair it with a sandwich or hearty salad. Packed with aroma and flavor, it's also delicious warmed up the second day.

SERVES 4

1 teaspoon peanut or vegetable oil

1 red bell pepper, diced

1 teaspoon minced ginger

1 clove garlic, minced

1 small chili pepper, finely diced

1½ cups frozen corn

2 cups coconut milk beverage (do not use canned coconut milk)

1 teaspoon prepared red curry paste

¼ teaspoon salt (optional)

1 medium tomato, chopped

½ cup chopped fresh cilantro

1 lime, quartered

2 green onions, sliced

Heat oil in a medium pot. Sauté bell pepper, ginger, garlic, and chili pepper in pot over medium-high for 8 minutes.

Stir in corn, coconut milk beverage, red curry paste, salt (optional), and tomato. Heat over medium-high while stirring, until bubbling and heated through, about 4 minutes.

Dish up bowls of soup and garnish as desired with cilantro, fresh lime, and green onions (you can also place cilantro, lime, and green onions in a serving dish and allow guests to garnish their soup as they prefer).

Nutrition information per serving: 112 calories, 4 g total fat, 2 g saturated fat, 0 mg cholesterol, 20 mg sodium, 18 g carbohydrates, 3 g fiber, 3 g sugar, 3 g protein

12

Berkeley Frame
of Mind

The university town of Berkeley has always been a beacon for the counterculture, especially when it comes to the food system. This is home to key movers and shakers in the good food movement, such as Michael Pollan and Alice Waters, who have been talking about the benefits of a slower, more plant-based and local food system for decades. But long before you read your first Michael Pollan book, or thumbed through an Alice Waters cookbook, an alternative food movement had been incubating in the East Bay.

There was even a hippie movement called the Berkeley Food Conspiracy in 1969, which was a network of households and communes who would pool their money to buy large supplies of goods, such as vegetables, grains, and peanut butter. The group would meet up to divide the food, and while they were together, they started having conversations about society and politics. Sure, it was essentially a co-op, but they liked the term "conspiracy" so much better.

Lush heirloom tomatoes in every color of the rainbow grown by local farmers in the sunny climate of California.

After San Francisco's "Summer of Love," one of the hallmarks of the hippie scene was that element of rising against social norms and getting back to the land to experience a gentler lifestyle that bucked consumerism. Communes arose around Berkeley, just 14 miles away from San Francisco, where the gentle climate and fertile soils could support all manner of crops, so, naturally they started growing their own food.

About the same time, a young Berkeley resident named Frances Moore Lappé began observing that the current food system based on livestock agriculture was destroying the planet, and a vegetarian diet might help alleviate that. To this day, her 1971 book, *Diet for a Small Planet*, has been the inspiration for countless people to take on a plant-based diet. In fact, the history of the vegetarian movement in America owes its start, in many ways, to this community.

A new peaceful, flower child food aesthetic arose from this movement, which favored the use of whole grains, vegetables, fermented foods, and pulses. The concept of killing animals for human luxury was reviled; in its place was ushered in an appreciation for Eastern proteins, such as tofu, tempeh, and seitan. And while they were at it, why not integrate other food traditions, such as African, Middle Eastern, and Indian. While the rest of American cuisine during this period was about as bland and boring as Salisbury steak with boiled potatoes and canned peas, the hippie food culture celebrated global herbs and spices, like cumin and turmeric, hummus, and curry. While mainstream America ate its doughy white Wonder bread, the folks in Berkeley fermented their own sourdough starter to bake up rough, whole grain breads. They drizzled their salads with tahini, and piled alfalfa sprouts and avocados onto their veggie sandwiches. They mixed up their own vegetarian nut and lentil loaves as a send-up to American meat loaf. There wasn't a dish that couldn't be made better with the addition of cooked sweet potatoes. They stirred nutritional yeast (nooch) into popcorn, and wheat germ and mashed bananas into sugar-free whole grain muffins. They basically invented granola. It was all about natural, healthful, organic ingredients that were beautiful in their simplicity.

Getting Hippy with It

Think like a hippie when you're eating, if just a little bit. It will bring an air of gentle, peaceful innocence, as well as health and flower power to your life.

- Try sprouting some beans (mung, alfalfa, and lentil), and use them in your salads, wraps, and sandwiches.

- Learn to love nutritional yeast, which is delicious in faux cheese sauces, popcorn, and tofu scrambles.

- Get a little crunchy, granola. Go deep into whole grain, seeded breads, put avocados on everything, pile on the home-cooked beans and tofu, and sprinkle hemp seeds all over the place.

Green CBD Oil Smoothie

Try a super-groovy green smoothie, naturally sweetened with bananas and powered with leafy greens, avocados, hemp, and CBD oil. While the jury is still out on many of the health advantages proclaimed for CBD, some research documents its potential benefits in improving sleep; relieving symptoms of arthritis, epilepsy, and chronic pain; and reducing anxiety and depression. So, go ahead and whip up this healthy, delicious smoothie for a light meal or snack.

SERVES 1

1 cup packed greens (kale, chard, spinach)

1 medium banana

17 mg CBD per CBD oil (see *Note*)

2 tablespoons hemp seeds

½ small avocado

¾ cup soymilk, plain, unsweetened (may substitute another type of protein-rich plant-based milk)

1 teaspoon lemon juice

Place all ingredients in a blender and process a few minutes until smooth and creamy.

Pour into a large glass and enjoy!

Note: There is no firmly established dose for CBD, but some people may find benefits with as little as 3 mg of CBD, while others may take 25–40 mg per day. Please read the label of your CBD oil to see the recommended amount of CBD per dosage—it can range from a few drops to a full dropper to get this amount, depending on the product. If the bottle doesn't list how much CBD is contained per dropper, but lists how much CBD is in the full bottle, then simply divide the total mg of CBD in the bottle by servings per bottle to determine the amount. For example, if a bottle contains 500 mg CBD, and there are thirty droppersful per bottle, then each dropper contains about 17 mg of CBD. In this recipe, you can use the dosage you prefer for one serving, but 17 mg is a fairly common daily dosage. As with all dietary supplements, you should discuss the use of CBD with your physician before you start a new regimen.

Nutrition information per serving: 472 calories, 28 g total fat, 3 g saturated fat, 0 mg cholesterol, 102 mg sodium, 47 g carbohydrates, 16 g sugar, 13 g fiber, 17 g protein

Tahini Swirl Brownies with Hemp

While tahini seems to be having its moment, it's actually a traditional ingredient made from ground sesame seeds used in Middle Eastern dishes for centuries. And it's also long been appreciated in the health food stores of Berkeley as the plant-powered superfood it really is. Rich in protein, fiber, healthy fats, and minerals, including calcium, this earthy spread offers a unique flavor to numerous dishes, including these dark chocolate, low-sugar, nutritious brownies.

SERVES 16

For the brownies:

½ cup nut meal (peanut, almond, hazelnut)

⅓ cup cocoa powder

2 tablespoons flaxseeds

2 tablespoons hemp seeds

½ cup coconut palm sugar (or brown sugar)

1½ teaspoons baking powder

9 medium dates, pitted

½ cup tahini

1 teaspoon vanilla

1 cup plant-based milk, plain, unsweetened

½ cup dairy-free chocolate chips

For the topping:

2 tablespoons tahini

2 tablespoons pure maple syrup

1½ teaspoons hemp seeds

Preheat oven to 350°F.

In the container of a blender or food processor, place nut meal, cocoa powder, flaxseeds, 2 tablespoons hemp seeds, sugar, baking powder, dates, ½ cup tahini, vanilla, and plant-based milk. Process until smooth on high setting, about 2 minutes, pausing to scrape down sides as needed.

Remove lid and stir in chocolate chips by hand with a wooden spoon.

Spray a 9 × 9-inch baking dish with nonstick cooking spray.

Pour batter into the baking dish and spread out evenly.

To make the topping, mix the 2 tablespoons tahini with the maple syrup in a small dish.

Drizzle the topping over the brownies, and then gently swirl the surface with a knife. Sprinkle with hemp seeds.

Place baking dish in the oven and bake for 40–45 minutes, until fork inserted in center comes out clean.

Cool for 10 minutes. Slice into sixteen brownies.

Nutrition information per serving: 151 calories, 6 g total fat, 2 g saturated fat, 0 mg cholesterol, 10 mg sodium, 26 g carbohydrates, 3 g fiber, 21 g sugar, 3 g protein

Curried Chickpea Quinoa Loaf

This vibrantly flavored, savory entrée is a modern, globally inspired take on a folksy, plant-based, meatless loaf with a reverent nod to the classic Indian dish Chana Masala. I love quirky plant-based loaves—essentially "meat loaves" without the meat. I grew up on these veggie loaves when I was a young girl, as they were classic fare among vegetarians in the sixties and seventies in the Northwest, as well as Berkeley. These meatless loaves really provide that savory quality to a meal that you might be craving—especially if you're new to plant-based eating. This recipe for Curried Chickpea Quinoa Loaf is fabulous for a comfort food dinner, holiday meal, or potluck. And I have to say that this recipe is one of my favorites—it is so bright and packed with flavors and aromas that are off the charts.

SERVES 6

For the loaf:

1 small onion, quartered

1 small (about 1–2 inches) fresh turmeric root, chopped (or 1 teaspoon dried turmeric)

2 cloves garlic

1 small (about 1 inch) fresh ginger root, chopped

1 cup mushrooms

1 cup coarsely chopped fresh greens (chard, spinach, kale), packed

2 tablespoons chopped fresh parsley or cilantro

2 tablespoons chia seeds

⅓ cup cashews

1 teaspoon garam masala*

½ teaspoon cumin

¼ teaspoon red chili flakes

½ cup cooked quinoa

1 15-ounce can chickpeas, drained

½ cup old-fashioned oats, uncooked

½ cup tomato sauce, canned

Place onion, turmeric root, garlic, ginger, mushrooms, greens, parsley, chia seeds, and cashews in a food processor and process just until chopped. Do not overprocess. Add 1 teaspoon garam masala, ½ teaspoon cumin, ¼ teaspoon red chili flakes, quinoa, chickpeas, oats, and ½ cup tomato sauce. Process just until chopped; do not overprocess or liquefy. (If you don't have a food processor, you can chop all ingredients very finely by hand and mix together in a large mixing bowl.)

Spray a loaf pan or narrow casserole dish with nonstick cooking spray and transfer the mixture to the pan or dish. Press contents into the pan or dish firmly. Place in the refrigerator and chill for about 1 hour.

Preheat oven to 350°F and bake for 50–60 minutes, until golden brown and firm. Allow to cool slightly before slicing it into thick slices.

While loaf is cooking make the sauce: Mix 1 cup tomato sauce with remaining pinch turmeric, ½ teaspoon garam masala, pinch cumin, and pinch red chili flakes and heat in a small pot until warmed through.

For the sauce:

1 cup tomato sauce, canned

Pinch turmeric

½ teaspoon garam masala*

Pinch cumin

Pinch red chili flakes

For the garnish:

1 teaspoon fresh, chopped
   parsley

Pour sauce over loaf, and garnish with chopped parsley.

*Note: Garam masala is a common Indian spice blend that can be found in specialty shops or online.

Nutrition information per serving: 194 calories, 6 g fat, 1 g saturated fat, 17 mg sodium, 0 mg cholesterol, 30 g carbohydrates, 7 g fiber, 5 g sugar, 8 g protein

Tree Hugger Breakfast Cookies

Creating sweet treats, without all of the added sugars, but with an ample supply of healthy whole grains, fruits, nuts, and seeds, is pure, sweet hippie love. These Tree Hugger Breakfast Cookies are bursting with nut butters, whole wheat flour, oats, seeds, nuts, and raisins. In fact, they are so healthy you can saddle up to one for breakfast without feeling a shred of regret! They are the perfect home-made breakfast for on-the-go eating. Kids will love them in their lunch boxes, too.

SERVES 24

2 tablespoons chia seeds

½ cup plant-based milk, plain, unsweetened

1 teaspoon vanilla

¼ cup dairy-free margarine spread

½ cup creamy peanut butter or almond butter

½ cup coconut palm sugar (or brown sugar)

1½ cups old-fashioned oats

1 cup whole wheat flour

1 teaspoon baking soda

½ teaspoon baking powder

2 tablespoons hemp seeds

2 tablespoons flaxseeds, ground

1 tablespoon sesame seeds

¼ cup pumpkin seeds

½ cup sliced almonds

½ cup chopped walnuts

½ cup raisins

½ cup dairy-free dark chocolate chips

Preheat oven to 350°F.

Place chia seeds in plant-based milk and whisk together for 2 minutes using an electric mixer.

Mix in vanilla, dairy-free margarine, and peanut or almond butter, using an electric mixer, until blended well.

Add coconut palm sugar, oats, flour, baking soda, baking powder, hemp seeds, flaxseeds, sesame seeds, pumpkin seeds, almonds, and walnuts, blending until smooth and combined well. Should make a crumbly mixture that holds together when pressed with hands.

Stir in raisins and chocolate chips using a wooden spoon.

Form cookie dough into golf-ball-sized balls with your hands, pressing together firmly, and place on baking sheet, allowing space for cookies to spread out slightly.

With a fork, press down on cookies to flatten slightly.

Bake for 20–25 minutes, until golden and firm.

Makes about two dozen large cookies.

Nutrition information per serving (1 cookie): 208 calories, 11 g total fat, 3 g saturated fat, 0 mg cholesterol, 77 mg sodium, 23 g carbohydrates, 4 g fiber, 10 g sugar, 6 g protein

Heirloom Bean Cassoulet with Root Vegetables

California cuisine celebrates the bounty that is local agriculture in combination with cultural culinary food traditions from this melting pot of the world. This golden place for agriculture also is known for its cultivation of heirloom beans—especially beautiful varieties of beans that farmers discovered during their harvest, saving the seeds back to plant the following year. Like a beautiful old quilt, these colorful, special beans are essentially heirlooms! Maybe it was an offshoot from a crop with a pretty color or especially vivid form—whatever it was, the farmer selected that one plant to harvest its beans (which are also seeds) and plant them again, forever preserving the unique qualities of that plant. That's why we have so many gorgeous, unique varieties of beans today! In this recipe, I use mint green flageolet beans, which I picked up in the East Bay area. However, you can use any type of heirloom or ordinary bean in this simple, crusty, French-style recipe, cooked with root vegetables.

SERVES 8

1 pound dried heirloom beans (flageolet, rattlesnake, calypso, or eye of the goat) or Great Northern beans

6 cups water

1 cube vegetable bouillon

2 bay leaves

½ teaspoon celery salt

3 medium garlic cloves, chopped

1 onion, coarsely chopped

2 carrots, coarsely sliced

1 parsnip, coarsely sliced

½ tablespoon extra-virgin olive oil

⅓ cup Mediterranean olives (Italian, Greek, Sicilian)

4 sprigs fresh rosemary

Soak beans in water overnight. Drain and rinse the beans and place in a large oven-safe pot or Dutch oven.

Add water, vegetable bouillon, bay leaves, celery salt, and garlic cloves and bring to a boil.

Reduce the heat to medium, cover, and simmer for 20 minutes.

Add onions, carrots, and parsnips, cover, and simmer for approximately 1 hour, until beans and vegetables are tender.

Preheat oven to 375°F.

Drizzle beans in pot with olive oil and top with olives and rosemary.

Place pot or Dutch oven on top rack of oven and bake for 10 minutes, uncovered.

Serve immediately.

Nutrition information per serving: 197 calories, 1 g total fat, 0 g saturated fat, 0 mg cholesterol, 77 mg sodium, 41 g carbohydrates, 13 g fiber, 7 g sugar, 14 g protein

Sweet Potato Corn Salad

Who says a delicious potato salad has to be focused only on the trademark ingredients of white potatoes, pickle relish, and mayo! This salad creation pairs unique, colorful plant foods—sweet potatoes, corn, pulses, greens, tomatoes, herbs, spices—to create an earth-loving, hearty salad you can bring to picnics, parties, and simple weekend gatherings. It also pays homage to local, indigenous food traditions, such as dishes made with maize (corn), black beans, local herbs and spices, and citrus—all things that grow so spectacularly in California. The spicy lime vinaigrette pairs well with the wholesome crunch of corn, beans, kale, and bell peppers. And it stores well for a couple of days in the refrigerator. It's pretty much a one-dish meal too, providing healthy carbs, protein, fiber, fats, vitamins, and minerals in one bowl.

SERVES 6

For the salad:

2 medium sweet potatoes, peeled, cubed

1 avocado, peeled, diced

1 cup cherry tomatoes (yellow, red, orange), halved

1 cup fire-roasted corn, frozen, defrosted

1 15-ounce can black beans, drained, rinsed

½ red onion, diced

1 bell pepper (green, red, yellow, orange), diced

½ cup fresh cilantro leaves, chopped

4 cups fresh kale, finely chopped

For the chili lime vinaigrette:

2 limes, juiced

1½ tablespoons extra-virgin olive oil

1 teaspoon agave syrup

2 cloves garlic, minced

½ teaspoon chili powder

½ teaspoon smoked paprika

¼ teaspoon red chili flakes

Sea salt (optional)

Place sweet potatoes in a small pot with water and cook until just tender but firm (about 15 minutes). Drain and place in a large mixing bowl, allowing to cool.

When cool, add avocado, tomatoes, corn, beans, onion, bell pepper, cilantro, and kale to potato mixture, combining gently.

For the vinaigrette: Whisk together all dressing ingredients in a small bowl and toss into potato corn mixture.

Serve immediately or chill until serving time.

Nutrition information per serving: 197 calories, 1 g total fat, 0 g saturated fat, 0 mg cholesterol, 77 mg sodium, 41 g carbohydrates, 13 g fiber, 7 g sugar, 14 g protein

13

Silicon Valley Startups

California's Silicon Valley is the epicenter of the high-tech plant-based future. Inventive companies are launching plant-based products left and right in this smart, savvy California locale, virtually disrupting the animal foods industry. You'd have to live under a rock to miss out on what companies in this area have done to the plant-based food industry and vegan food scene. Like Impossible Foods, with their now ubiquitous "bleeding" Impossible Burgers, and Just, maker of vegan Just Mayo and Just Eggs. Now it's sexy to say you tried a vegan burger at a fast food restaurant—even if you're a guy and a carnivore. And nearly every restaurant chain is jockeying to get a plant-based burger on its menu. You can walk into a Blaze Pizza anywhere across the country and order a vegan pizza, or stop at a Del Taco to get plant-based tacos starring vegan crumbles. Heck, you can even go to KFC to grub down some vegan fried chicken.

What's more, Silicon Valley is not just doing the food science work to create these vegan foods, they are infusing capital into new plant-based startups, whether it's Memphis Meats, which aims to remove animal

A plant-based table groaning with abundance, featuring some of the unique, delicious foods grown and enjoyed in California.

products from meat production, or Beyond Meat, a plant-based meat alternative infiltrating supermarkets, foodservice, and restaurants—even across the pond.

After all, who better to solve the high-tech question of the day, such as how to make a vegan egg without chickens? How to create a burger that tastes and smells like meat without a cow? How to create faux tuna that tastes of the sea? How to create a vegan collagen to replace animal-derived collagen from bones? The answers are all being created in the vibrant think tank of the new plant-based food industry, where ingredients, from nuts to seeds to algae, are being explored as potential new plant-based ingredients, offering a far more sustainable future than animal proteins.

What's the appeal? From Bill Gates to Leonardo DiCaprio to James Cameron, there is a legitimate passion for healing the planet and reducing the impact of climate change through investing in the future of the food system. So, why not put your money where your mouth is, literally?

And it's not just high-tech meat alternatives that have been fueling the vegan revolution. Amy's Kitchen, located not far from Silicon Valley, has been creating delicious plant-based frozen meals and canned foods like bowls and soups for adoring fans since 1983—they even have an Amy's Drive Thru in Rohnert Park. Nearby, the "queen of vegan cheese," Miyoko Schinner, has been crafting aged, French-style vegan cheeses since the 1980s. Not far away, Kelly and Brian Swette founded Sweet Earth Foods, starting with addictive plant-based wraps and breakfast burritos filled with seitan. All of these companies have gone from small, local darlings to major food companies commanding national attention.

Being plant-based today offers a modern world of culinary exploration and experience. Every week finds a new product popping up on shelves or menus, such as pistachio milk, chickpea "ice cream," and aquafaba (bean liquid) cocktails. More plant-based-only restaurants open up in cities every day, even across the planet (Berlin is the unofficial vegan capital of the world these days). And more mainstream restaurants, from Red Robin to The Cheesecake Factory, offer vegan menu options. You can also access new-world solutions for discovering plant-based foods, such as rideshare apps that allow you to search for vegan meal deliveries, and Happy Cow, the app that shares plant-based restaurant offerings near you from all over the world.

While the greatest benefits come from eating a diet based on whole plant foods—whole grains like oats, pulses like navy beans and black-eyed peas, a rainbow of vegetables and fruits, nuts and seeds like walnuts and pumpkin seeds—these modern meat alternatives offer an easy, delicious way to include more plant foods in your diet. Best of all, the plant-based revolution is introducing veganism to the masses—a good thing for people, animals, and the planet.

Modernize Your Plant-Based Eating Style

Go ahead and get techy with your plant-based eating.

- Try the new faux meats available in your market so you can pinpoint your favorites.

- Get gleeful when you spy a new plant-based product. Maybe it's a new brand of aged nut cheese. Or perhaps it's a new frozen entrée from Amy's Kitchen. Just grab it and grin.

- Don't be a food snob. Walk into a fast food restaurant you would've never stepped into and order a vegan meal. Ensure a continued demand for growth in the rapidly changing world of plant-based innovation.

Barbecue Pulled Jackfruit Sandwich with Apple Fennel Slaw

Though jackfruit—a staple plant crop in tropical countries, such as Southeast Asia—has been around for millennia, appearing in traditional foods of the region, it's become something of a plant-based darling in the US in recent years. That's because when the fruit is cooked, it forms strands, similar to pulled meat. You can find all sorts of newfangled plant-based jackfruit products in natural food stores today. But my favorite is a home-cooked pulled jackfruit, with my own favorite barbecue sauce. Cook the pulled jackfruit in this rich, flavorful sauce, and serve it on whole grain buns piled with my delicious, crunchy Apple Fennel Slaw. This is such a great outdoor meal for picnics, parties, or holidays. The leftovers are just as good, too.

SERVES 6

For the barbecue sauce:

¼ cup tomato paste

¼ cup ketchup

2 tablespoons apple cider vinegar

1 tablespoon dark molasses

3 tablespoons reduced sodium soy sauce

1 teaspoon whole grain mustard

1 teaspoon liquid smoke

1 teaspoon smoked paprika

1 teaspoon cumin

3 garlic cloves, minced

½ jalapeño pepper, finely diced

½ small white onion, finely diced

Salt (optional, as desired)

To prepare the barbecue sauce: In a medium bowl, mix together tomato paste, ketchup, vinegar, molasses, and soy sauce until smooth. Stir in whole grain mustard, liquid smoke, paprika, cumin, minced garlic cloves, finely diced jalapeño pepper, and finely diced white onion.

Season as desired with salt (optional). Set aside.

To prepare the pulled jackfruit: Pull apart the pieces of jackfruit with your fingers to create small stringy sections of fruit. For the dense cores and seeds, pinch them apart with your fingers to create smaller pieces.

Heat oil in a large sauté pan or Dutch oven. Add onions and sauté for 8 minutes.

Add jackfruit to the cooked onions and sauté for 3 minutes.

For the pulled jackfruit:

1 20-ounce can jackfruit, drained, reserve liquid

1 teaspoon extra-virgin olive oil

1 small onion, diced

½ cup reserved jackfruit liquid

Water, as needed

6 whole grain hamburger buns, vegan, toasted

3 cups Apple Fennel Slaw (page 130)

Add barbecue sauce and ½ cup of the reserved jackfruit liquid to the pan or Dutch oven, mix well, cover, and simmer for 20–25 minutes, stirring occasionally. Add additional water as needed to create a thick, moist texture.

To serve: Scoop ½ cup of the barbecue pulled jackfruit mixture on bottom of bun. Scoop ½ cup of Apple Fennel Slaw on top. Cover with top hamburger bun.

Serve immediately.

Nutrition information per serving: 361 calories, 6 g total fat, 1 g saturated fat, 0 mg cholesterol, 752 mg sodium, 71 g carbohydrates, 9 g fiber, 15 g sugar, 10 g protein

Vegan Eggplant Parmigiana

Fueling the plant-based revolution is the simple quest to replace classic animal-based ingredients in favorite dishes. Vegan cheese has always been one of the most highly sought after replacements in the plant-based world. And, oh how vegan cheeses have risen to the top! You can find award-winning plant-based cheeses today that can replace everything from brie to blue cheese to goat cheese. But, in my mind, nothing can replace the simple basic quality of a home-made cashew cream cheese, which has been whipped up by innovative home cooks for decades. In this super easy eggplant parmigiana, layers of eggplant, herbal marinara sauce, and home-made cashew cream cheese meld together into a crave-worthy comfort food.

SERVES 4

For the cashew cream cheese:

1 cup cashews, raw

½ cup plant-based milk, plain, unsweetened

½ small lemon, juiced

1 clove garlic

Pinch kosher salt and white pepper (optional)

1 tablespoon nutritional yeast

For the eggplant:

1 large eggplant

1 tablespoon extra-virgin olive oil

¼ teaspoon kosher salt

2 tablespoons whole grain breadcrumbs

For the herbed marinara sauce:

2 cups marinara sauce

1 clove garlic, minced

1 teaspoon basil

1 teaspoon oregano

Pinch black pepper

To make the cashew cream cheese: Place cashews in a bowl and cover with water. Soak for 1 hour. Drain cashews. Place cashews in a blender with plant-based milk, lemon juice, garlic, salt and white pepper (optional), and nutritional yeast. Process cashews until very smooth. May have to pause and scrape down sides a few times. Texture should be thick and creamy.

To make the eggplant: Preheat oven to 400°F on the broiler setting. Chop eggplant into thin vertical slices and place on a baking sheet. Drizzle with olive oil and sprinkle evenly with salt and breadcrumbs. Place in oven on top rack and broil for 8 minutes, until golden. Remove from oven and reduce heat to 375°F on the bake setting.

To make the herbed marinara sauce: Mix marinara sauce with garlic, basil, oregano, and black pepper in a small bowl.

To assemble: In a 9 × 9-inch baking dish, place ½ cup marinara sauce on the bottom and spread out evenly. Layer half the roasted eggplant on top of the marinara sauce, followed by half the remaining marinara sauce, and half the cashew cream. Repeat layers one more time with remaining ingredients. Place uncovered in 375°F oven and bake for 30 minutes. Remove, allow to cool for 5 minutes, slice into squares, and serve.

Nutrition information per serving: 215 calories, 8 g total fat, 1 g saturated fat, 352 mg sodium, 36 g carbohydrates, 9 g fiber, 5 g sugar, 4 g protein

Yellow Squash, Cilantro, Soy Chorizo Pizza on Whole Grain Flax Crust

Have you seen how many fabulous vegan pizzas are available in natural food stores and restaurants these days? But my favorite plant-based pizzas are the ones I make myself, with this fabulous, crunchy, whole grain flax crust (page 213), and layers of veggie toppings. This colorful pizza has a decidedly Latin flavor profile, compliments of the soy chorizo, yellow squash, cilantro, and jalapeño. It also shows off the current innovations in the plant-based world, such as soy-based meat alternatives, and vegan cheese in flavors and textures that actually melt on the crust.

SERVES 8 (1 14-INCH PIZZA)

1 Whole Grain Flax Pizza Crust (page 213)

2 teaspoons cornmeal

For the pizza toppings:

½ cup marinara sauce

1 cup shredded plant-based cheese, mozzarella flavor

1 small yellow squash, thinly sliced

1 6-ounce package soy chorizo, prepared

1 small jalapeño, sliced

2 cloves garlic, minced

2 green onions, sliced

½ cup fresh cilantro

Prepare one Whole Grain Flax Pizza Crust.

Preheat oven to 400°F.

Sprinkle a pizza stone or baking sheet with cornmeal. Place rolled out pizza dough on the pizza stone or baking sheet.

Cover pizza dough with marinara sauce, evenly smoothing over surface.

Sprinkle evenly with plant-based cheese.

Arrange sliced yellow squash evenly over surface.

Remove soy chorizo from package and pinch off or crumble small pieces to arrange evenly over the pizza.

Arrange sliced jalapeño over pizza.

Sprinkle with garlic.

Place pizza on top rack of oven and bake for about 30–35 minutes, until golden brown and cooked through.

Remove pizza from oven and sprinkle evenly with green onions and cilantro. Slice into eight wedges and serve immediately.

Nutrition information per serving: 177 calories, 7 g total fat, 1 g saturated fat, 0 mg cholesterol, 25 g carbohydrates, 6 g fiber, 4 g sugar, 8 g protein

Whole Grain Flax Pizza Crust

Make your own yeasty, crispy pizza crust with this trusty whole grain recipe. Just get the dough ready, then top it with your favorite assortment of veggie toppings, such as pizza or marinara sauce, plant-based cheese, onions, mushrooms, squash, peppers, sweet potatoes, leafy greens, cauliflower, broccoli, herbs, spices, nuts, and seeds. I even like to put a salad on top of a prepared pizza to fit more fresh veggies into my day. One of my favorite pizza recipes is the Latin-themed Yellow Squash, Cilantro, Soy Chorizo Pizza on page 210. Double up on the recipe to make two at a time—the leftovers are always welcome.

SERVES 8 (1 14-INCH PIZZA CRUST)

¾ cup warm water (110°F)

1¼-ounce package active dry yeast

½ teaspoon agave syrup

1½ teaspoons extra-virgin olive oil

1½ cups whole wheat flour (plus additional for kneading and rolling out)

¼ cup ground flaxseeds

Pinch salt (optional)

2 teaspoons cornmeal

In a medium bowl, stir together the water, yeast, and agave. Let stand for 10 minutes.

Stir in the olive oil, flour, flaxseeds, and salt (optional). Turn out dough onto a floured surface and knead for about 10 minutes, until smooth, yet slightly sticky.

Place the dough in an oiled bowl, cover with a towel, and place in a warm (but not hot) place for 1 hour, until doubled in size.

Preheat oven to 400°F.

Punch the dough down with your hand and roll it out on a floured surface to about 14 inches in diameter.

Sprinkle cornmeal on a pizza stone or pan or baking sheet. Place pizza dough on pizza stone or pan or baking sheet. Top as desired. Bake until crust is golden brown and toppings are cooked through.

Nutrition information per serving: 113 calories, 7 g total fat, 1 g saturated fat, 0 mg cholesterol, 246 mg sodium, 26 g carbohydrates, 6 g fiber, 4 g sugar, 8 g protein.

Warm Sesame Shitake Mushroom Tofu Salad

Tofu is a traditional, minimally processed plant protein that's been around for centuries in diets from many countries in Asia. I've seen firsthand how tofu is made in California, where a variety of companies make this classic plant ingredient, including the Bay Area company Hodo Tofu, which has grown in popularity for its artisanal tofu-making skills. Tofu is simply soybeans, cooked and filtered into soymilk, which is then coagulated to form a curd. That's it! This umami bomb of a salad features a warm sauté of tofu and shitake served over greens to give them a savory yet tender treatment.

SERVES 4

1 tablespoon sesame oil

4 ounces fresh shitake mushrooms, sliced

1 clove garlic, minced

8 ounces extra firm tofu, drained, cubed

Pinch red pepper flakes

1 tablespoon reduced sodium soy sauce, gluten-free

1 tablespoon orange juice

1 teaspoon rice vinegar

4 cups chopped kale

2 green onions, sliced

1 tablespoon sesame seeds

Heat oil in a small skillet.

Add mushrooms, garlic, and tofu. Sauté for 2 minutes.

Stir in red pepper flakes, soy sauce, orange juice, and rice vinegar, and sauté for an additional 2–3 minutes, until mushrooms are tender and golden.

Place chopped kale in a salad bowl. Add the warm mushroom tofu mixture and liquid in the pan and toss together lightly.

Garnish with green onions and sesame seeds.

Serve immediately, while warm.

Nutrition information per serving: 167 calories, 10 g total fat, 1 g saturated fat, 316 mg sodium, 0 mg cholesterol, 11 g carbohydrates, 5 g fiber, 3 g sugar, 13 g protein

Beet Bean Veggie Burgers with Sriracha Caramelized Onions

Trendy veggie burgers "bleed" on the bun and come so close to meat, you can barely tell the difference. Viva la plant-based innovation! However, you can get your own version of innovation on in your home kitchen with these beet bean veggie burgers that are red, compliments of beets. These flavorful burgers are filled with plant protein, fiber, and antioxidant compounds, plus they are potent in taste, especially with those sriracha caramelized onions piled on the burger.

SERVES 8

For the beet bean veggie burgers:

3 fresh medium beets (about 3 ounces each), unpeeled, trimmed, scrubbed with a vegetable brush

6 medium brown mushrooms

1 small onion

3 cloves garlic

1 15-ounce can red kidney beans, rinsed, drained

¾ cup old-fashioned oats, dry

2 tablespoons ground flaxseeds

½ cup finely chopped pecans

2 tablespoons reduced sodium soy sauce

2 tablespoons lemon juice

1½ teaspoons cumin

1½ teaspoons smoked paprika

1 teaspoon oregano

Salt, as desired (optional)

To make the beet bean veggie burgers: Using a food processor with shredder disk, shred beets, mushrooms, 1 small onion, and 3 cloves garlic into the container of the food processor. (If you don't have a food processor, use a box grater and grate vegetables by hand.)

Place kidney beans in a large mixing bowl and mash with a potato masher until smooth with some small chunks visible.

Add the shredded beets, mushrooms, onion, and garlic to the mixing bowl with beans.

Add oats, flaxseeds, pecans, soy sauce, lemon juice, cumin, paprika, and oregano to the mixing bowl. Combine well, using clean hands to mix if necessary. Should make a thick, moist mixture. Season with salt according to preference. Cover and refrigerate at least 1 hour (or overnight).

Preheat oven to 350°F.

Spray a baking sheet with nonstick cooking spray.

Using a ½-cup measuring cup, scoop up ½ cup of mixture and transfer to the baking sheet. Pat down to create round veggie burgers about ¾ inch thick. Makes eight veggie burgers.

Place on the top rack of the oven and bake for about 50–55 minutes, until cooked through. Remove from oven.

**For the sriracha
caramelized onions:**

1 tablespoon sesame oil

3 medium onions, sliced

2 cloves garlic, minced

1–2 teaspoons sriracha (per
taste preference)

Salt, as desired (optional)

**For the toppings
and buns:**

8 whole grain hamburger
buns, toasted

½ cup vegan mayo (optional)

½ cup whole grain mustard
(optional)

To make the sriracha caramelized onions: Heat sesame oil in a large
skillet or saucepan over medium heat and add onions and garlic, sautéing for about 20–25 minutes, until golden brown.

Season with sriracha sauce and salt per your preference.

To serve: Place cooked burgers on toasted buns, drizzle with vegan
mayo and/or mustard (if desired), and top with caramelized onions.

Nutrition information per serving: 380 calories, 11 g total fat, 1 g saturated
fat, 558 mg sodium, 0 mg cholesterol, 59 g carbohydrates, 13 g fiber, 9 g
sugar, 15 g protein

14

Soulful Roots

From plant-based athletes to the hottest celebrities (Beyonce, I'm talking about you), the plant-based movement is alive and well among the African-American community in California. The healthful, vegan movement has empowered people to take charge of their health and fight chronic diseases, including obesity, type 2 diabetes, and heart disease, that disproportionately impact Black lives and tear down families and communities. There is powerful value in reconnecting with the very roots of African food culture, which was brought to America through the traditions of African slaves, as they tilled the soil, planted the crops, and cooked their time-honored recipes. Some of the very genetic plant material that was grown in the South during this period came by way of the West Africans, who tucked away tiny precious seeds in their hair for safekeeping as they were rounded up for the slave ships.

We wouldn't even know so many classic American foods if it weren't for the culinary traditions given to us by the generations of African Americans, who learned how to cultivate plants and fold them into the fabric of American cuisine. Greens, black-eyed peas, rice—all came by way of West African foodways—even down to the way these foods were washed, cooked,

With its year-round growing season, there is always an abundance of fresh produce in California to inspire seasonal, plant-based eating.

and served. Other food influences were folded in along the way, such as French, Spanish, and Latin.

At the heart of this food style was a simple yet hearty cuisine that was based on what was available and abundant, and nothing went to waste. If an apple tree bowed with its heavy fruit, it was time to make pies and sauce. When the nuts fell from the tree, it was time to harvest, shell, and dry them for use all winter long in baking. The forest held an ample supply of wild greens and herbs—virtually medicine for what ails you—free for the taking. The kitchen garden and neighboring woods became the essence of nourishment to feed the body and soul.

In fact, the original, traditional diet from the African diaspora is about as healthful as you might find. A boost of leafy greens—one of the most nutritious foods on the planet—is at the diet's core, along with a medley of colorful local, seasonal, cultivated and foraged fruits and vegetables, such as papaya and breadfruit. Then comes a swath of hearty whole grains—millet, sorghum, teff, bulgur, rice—to provide a steady source of slow-digesting carbs. Proteins most often take the form of pulses such as pigeon peas and broadbeans, and seeds and nuts, like groundnuts and peanuts. An abundant use of flavorful spices and herbs, like cumin and coriander, accompany these foods. Dairy foods are not commonly consumed, and meat intake is low, as these foods are precious and often reserved for special occasions. Exercise is a part of daily life. Of course, each country and people have their own unique food traditions, and some parts of Africa have climates that don't favor growing crops like grains and vegetables. But the end result is an overall diet pattern that starkly departs from today's Western diet, filled with chips, soda, and burgers.

So, it's exciting to see a celebration of food traditions within the Black community and the embrace of a healthful, plant-based diet for health benefits. Ron Finley (aka the Gangsta Gardener) is planting urban gardens in deserted South LA lots to provide access to fruits and vegetables for all. Pro football player David Carter, known as the 300-pound vegan, and vegan bodybuilder Torre Washington are smashing stereotypes that athletes and "real men" have to eat meat in order to be strong. Following suit, Kareem Cook teamed up with John Lewis, known as the Bad Ass Vegan, to enter the vegan food business world, creating the successful VeganSmart brand of nutritional shakes. And Jay Z and Beyonce founded the Greenprint Project, which hopes to inspire more people to adopt a vegan-centric lifestyle. What do all of these leaders in the African-American community have in common? They are undoubtedly cool, and they are inspiring people in droves to take back control of their health, for people and the planet. These insightful leaders are also showing that healthy, plant-based fare can be full of soul and flavor.

Bringing Soul to Your Kitchen

No matter your cultural roots, we all have some traditional foods that satisfy our souls, worthy of embracing in a plant-based kitchen.

- Trace back beloved plant-based recipes within your family's culture. From simmered beans and greens to green bean casserole, the best foods in food cultures start out with plants.

- Don't skimp on flavor. There's no need to get wimpy when it comes to culinary additions to dishes that will make them shine. Case in point: garlic, cayenne, parsley, lemon juice. Bring it on!

- No need to go hungry. Plant-based eating goes beyond sprout wraps and lettuce leaf tacos. Satisfy your longing for really good food that sticks to your ribs, I'm talking whole grain breads, macaroni, beans, and stews.

Ethiopian Lentil Yam Stew with Turmeric Rice

One of the trademark virtues of Ethiopian cooking is the unique use of herbs and spices in savory dishes. While in the states you might limit sweet spices to baking, they shine regally in the country dishes of Ethiopia. In fact, if you get a chance, pinpoint your nearest Ethiopian restaurant, no matter where you live, and give it a try. You will find a whole world of delicious plant-based foods awaiting you from Sub-Saharan Africa, such as a spongy, fermented bread (injera) used to dip up every last drop of a legume stew like this one.

SERVES 8

For the turmeric rice:

1½ cups long grain brown rice, uncooked

4 cups water

1 teaspoon turmeric

Salt, as desired (optional)

For the stew:

1 tablespoon extra-virgin olive oil

1 large onion, diced

2 teaspoons grated fresh ginger

3 cloves garlic, minced

1 red bell pepper, diced

2 medium (about 5 ounces each) yams or sweet potatoes, peeled, cubed

¼ cup water

1 teaspoon paprika

½–1 teaspoon cayenne pepper (depending on your spiciness preference)

½ teaspoon coriander

¼ teaspoon allspice

¼ teaspoon cinnamon

½ teaspoon black pepper

1½ cups red lentils, uncooked

1 14.5-ounce can diced tomatoes, with juice

4 cups vegetable broth

Salt, as desired (optional)

2 cups chopped fresh greens (chard, spinach, mustard greens), packed

¼ cup chopped fresh mint leaves

To cook the turmeric rice: Add rice, water, turmeric, and salt (as desired) to a small pot, stir, cover, and bring to a simmer. Cook until tender (about 40 minutes). Drain any leftover water.

To make the stew: Heat olive oil in a large pot. Add onions and sauté for 4 minutes.

Add ginger, garlic, bell pepper, and yams or sweet potatoes, and sauté for an additional 1 minute.

Add water, paprika, cayenne pepper, coriander, allspice, cinnamon, and black pepper, and sauté for an additional 3 minutes.

Add lentils, tomatoes, and vegetable broth. Stir well, cover, and simmer for about 25–30 minutes, until the vegetables are tender, yet firm.

Season with salt, as desired. Stir in fresh greens and remove from heat, allowing the temperature of the stew to cook the greens.

Serve stew with rice, sprinkled with freshly chopped mint.

Makes about ½ cup rice with 1 cup stew per serving.

Nutrition information per serving: 296 calories, 3 g total fat, 0 g saturated fat, 0 mg cholesterol, 160 mg sodium, 55 g carbohydrates, 15 g fiber, 5 g sugar, 13 g protein

Couscous with Aubergine and Chickpeas

In North Africa, tiny pearls of wheat-based couscous are commonly served with rich, spiced tomato broth and local vegetables, including aubergine (eggplant) and chickpeas. The vegetable stew, seasoned with the traditional seasoning blend ras el hanout, *is often simmered in a tagine—a clay, cone-shaped cooking vessel used to cook foods over a flame— which does double duty as a serving dish.*

SERVES 6

For the couscous:

2¼ cups water

1½ cups whole wheat pearl couscous, uncooked

¼ teaspoon salt (optional)

1 teaspoon extra-virgin olive oil

For the eggplant and chickpeas:

2 tablespoons extra-virgin olive oil

1 large onion, diced

3 cloves garlic, minced

1 tablespoon *ras el hanout* (Moroccan seasoning blend)

1 large eggplant, diced

1 green bell pepper, diced

1 15-ounce can chickpeas, rinsed, drained

½ cup olives, pitted, drained

1 14.5-ounce can diced tomatoes, with juice

1 cup vegetable broth

¼ cup chopped fresh parsley

To make the couscous: Bring water to a boil, stir in couscous, salt (optional), and olive oil, cover, and reduce heat to medium. Cook for about 10 minutes, until just tender but firm. Remove from heat, drain any excess liquid, and keep covered. Just before serving, fluff with a fork.

To make the eggplant and chickpeas: Heat olive oil in a large sauté pan or skillet over medium heat.

Add onions and garlic and sauté for 4 minutes.

Add *ras el hanout* and sauté for 1 minute.

Add eggplant and bell pepper and sauté for 10 minutes.

Add chickpeas, olives, tomatoes, and broth, stirring well. Cover and simmer for 10–15 minutes, stirring frequently, until mixture is thick and vegetables are tender yet firm.

To serve: In a serving dish or individual serving bowls, arrange the couscous. Top with the aubergine and chickpeas mixture, and garnish with fresh parsley.

Makes about 3 cups couscous and 7 cups aubergine and chickpeas.

Nutrition information per serving: 375 calories, 9 g total fat, 1 g saturated fat, 0 mg cholesterol, 439 mg sodium, 64 g carbohydrates, 11 g fiber, 4 g sugar, 12 g protein

Broccoli Au Gratin

Vegetable side dishes are pure comfort, and part of many African-American food traditions that transcend to other regional foodways across the country. Whether it's for a Sunday night dinner, holiday, or simple home-cooked weeknight meal, these simple dishes can be the highlight of the entire table. Take this completely plant-based version of a classic broccoli au gratin, which features long-stem broccoli, walnuts, rosemary, and a plant-based cheese sauce.

SERVES 8

1½ pounds fresh long-stem broccoli or broccolini

For the walnut crumb mixture:

¼ cup whole wheat breadcrumbs

1 cup shredded sharp plant-based cheese, divided

½ cup coarsely chopped walnuts

1 tablespoon fresh rosemary (or 1 teaspoon dried)

1 tablespoon extra-virgin olive oil

For the sauce:

1 tablespoons extra-virgin olive oil

½ onion, diced

1 clove garlic, minced

2 tablespoons flour

¾ cup vegetable broth

1 cup plant-based milk, plain, unsweetened

½ teaspoon black pepper

Salt (optional)

Bring a medium pot of water to boil. Place broccoli in pot, cover, and cook for about 8 minutes, until just tender but bright green. Drain, and transfer cooked broccoli to a 9-inch casserole dish.

Preheat oven to 375°F.

Spray a baking dish or baking sheet with nonstick cooking spray. In a small bowl, combine breadcrumbs, ¼ cup shredded plant-based cheese, walnuts, rosemary, and 1 tablespoon olive oil, mixing well.

Place walnut crumb mixture in the baking dish or sheet and place on top rack of oven. Bake 15 minutes, until golden brown. Remove from oven and set aside.

Meanwhile, heat 1 tablespoon olive oil in a saucepan and add onions and garlic, sautéing for 5 minutes. Add flour and cook an additional minute. Stir in broth and plant-based milk and cook for an additional minute. Stir in ¾ cup plant-based cheese and black pepper, and heat until thick and creamy. Season with salt if desired.

Pour sauce evenly over broccoli in casserole dish. Sprinkle with walnut crumb mixture.

Serve immediately.

Nutrition information per serving: 197 calories, 14 g total fat, 4 g saturated fat, 15 mg cholesterol, 208 mg sodium, 13 g carbohydrates, 3 g fiber, 3 g sugar, 9 g protein

Easy Vegan Mashed Potatoes

Is there anything more comforting when you've had a long hard day, or even heading over to your mom's house for dinner, than a steaming bowl of freshly mashed potatoes? Yes, you can make vegan mashed potatoes as easily and deliciously (and much more healthfully) than standard dairy-based mashers, and this easy recipe is evidence. It is a foolproof classic that has graced my dinner table time and time again. Serve it with the Savory Mushroom Sauce on page 64 for a true slice of heaven.

SERVES 6

5 medium (6 ounces each) potatoes, peeled, halved

Water, as needed

1½ tablespoons dairy-free margarine

½–¾ cup plant-based milk, plain, unsweetened

Salt and pepper (optional)

Fill pot with water and bring to a boil. Add potatoes, cover, and cook until tender (about 30–35 minutes). The potatoes should be tender enough to pierce easily with a fork, but still retain their form.

Remove pot from heat, drain, and mash potatoes with a potato masher or electric mixer for just a few seconds.

Add dairy-free margarine, then gradually add enough plant-based milk, mixing with an electric mixer, to make a smooth, creamy mashed potato mixture, according to your texture preference. Season with and salt and pepper as desired. Serve immediately.

Nutrition information per serving: 165 calories, 3 g total fat, 1 g saturated fat, 21 mg sodium, 32 g carbohydrates, 2 g fiber, 2 g sugar, 4 g protein

Caribbean Coconut Rice with Okra

The African-Caribbean notes of spices, coconut, and okra infuse this fried rice side dish with unparalleled flavor. The shades of green against white make it a pretty addition to your dining room table, as well. It is fabulous served with a side of simple cooked red beans. Bring it to your next potluck for a huge hit. Or meal prep it to tote it along to work for a healthy, satisfying meal.

SERVES 4

For the coconut rice:

1 cup brown rice, short or long grain, uncooked

1 13.5-ounce can light coconut milk

½ cup water

For the okra sauté:

1 teaspoon peanut oil

½ small red onion, diced

1 small jalapeño pepper, finely diced

3 cloves garlic, minced

8 ounces fresh okra, sliced into 1-inch pieces (may use frozen)

3 tablespoons water

1 teaspoon allspice

1 teaspoon paprika

1 teaspoon thyme

¼ teaspoon black pepper

Salt (optional)

2 tablespoons shredded unsweetened coconut

2 tablespoons chopped fresh mint leaves

2 stalks green onions, sliced

Place brown rice in a small pot. Add coconut milk and ½ cup water, stir well, cover with lid, and simmer until liquid is absorbed and rice is just tender but not overcooked (35–45 minutes, depending on type of rice). Stir frequently while it is cooking so that it doesn't stick.

Meanwhile, heat peanut oil in a sauté pan or skillet and add diced red onion, jalapeño pepper, and garlic, sautéing for 5 minutes.

Add okra and sauté for 2 minutes.

Add 3 tablespoons water, allspice, paprika, thyme, black pepper, and salt (optional), and cook okra for an additional 6 minutes, until crisp tender.

Add cooked rice and sauté, stirring to blend together, for an additional 2 minutes, until okra is tender, but still bright green, and rice is golden.

Remove from heat. Stir in coconut and mint leaves. Garnish with green onions and serve immediately.

Nutrition information per serving: 292 calories, 10 g total fat, 5 g saturated fat, 0 mg cholesterol, 21 mg sodium, 46 g carbohydrates, 5 g fiber, 2 g sugar, 6 g protein

15

California Mediterranean

When you think of California regional foods, what instantly comes to mind? You might think of pretty trailing vineyards in the gorgeous Napa Valley, producing rich vibrant wines. Or cheerful citrus farms along the Southern Coast, with bushy limbs festooned with oranges resembling a decked-out Christmas tree dropping their juicy fruit. Perhaps you think of the stretches of farmland, with trucks humming down the dusty highway filled with garlic, walnuts, or tomatoes. Maybe you might even think of the gray-silver foliage of olive farms, producing some of the best olive oil in the world. And your musings would be absolutely right! What do all of these examples highlight? That California is one of the few Mediterranean growing regions in the world, thanks to its amazing ability to produce some of our most beloved plant foods on the planet: wines, olives, citrus, and

My favorite ingredients for a plant-based kitchen come from unusual varieties of plants, such as these heirloom garlic bulbs grown by a local farmer in Southern California.

nuts. And that's not all! You can add a rainbow of produce to the growing list, including avocados, artichokes, asparagus, berries, fennel, radishes, squash . . . the list goes on and on.

Many of these foods can only be grown in this special climate we know as the Mediterranean. The availability of these ingredients has deeply influenced and fused California's cuisine toward a decidedly Mediterranean bent. For years, California chefs have been ditching butter for olive oil. Skipped out on the creamy sauces and soups for broth-based, herbal infusions. They've visited local farms to get the very best of seasonal, newly harvested vegetables. And they've gone light on animal proteins in lieu of highlighting vegetables. They've always been on the lookout for a staple, from ancient grains to beluga lentils, to take the place of meat on the plate.

I've just described the Mediterranean diet for you, which is a diet based on the traditional and local foods of countries surrounding the Mediterranean Sea. In this sun-drenched part of the world lived primarily farmers, who learned to work the land to produce crops that craved the sunshine. Some of the hallmark facets of a Mediterranean diet include olive oil as the main fat, a diet primarily based on plants with low red meat intake, a rich variety of whole grains and pulses, a wide variety of seasonal, local vegetables and fruits, and wine enjoyed on a daily (moderate) basis. Check, check, check, check, and check!

The Mediterranean diet is much more than just ingredients. It is about a lifestyle, a *way* of eating. It is about growing some of your own food and visiting the weekly farm stands to handpick the best of the seasonal produce grown by your neighbors. It is about enjoying a leisurely, simple meal in the company of others, with a local bottle of wine to sip along with the meal, and laugh and cry over shared stories. And then going for a small walk in the village to help "digest" the food before retiring for the evening. The California Mediterranean aesthetic is moving its way toward these ideals too. Eating long, relaxed meals outdoors with friends and a bottle of wine is almost a religion for many! These concepts are all part of a rich lifestyle that can be enjoyed virtually anywhere.

Living the Mediterranean Life

Bring a touch of the healthy Mediterranean life to your kitchen.

- Make olive oil your number one oil. Sure, it might have to be imported, but some things are worth it.

- Enjoy wine with meals, in moderation. One glass a day for women and two for men is linked with health benefits as part of the Mediterranean diet.

- Celebrate the seasons. The heart of the Mediterranean diet is really the regional, seasonal produce. Sicilian tomatoes, artichokes as big as your head, capers that taste like the sea. Find the seasonal vegetable treasures in your own backyard, and honor them by serving them at your table.

Cretan-Style Lima Beans

At the very epicenter of the Mediterranean diet is the island of Crete in Greece. It is here—an isle filled with olive orchards and farms—that researchers identified health benefits and longevity related to the Mediterranean diet. One of my favorite traditional recipes from this region is a simple bean dish cooked in a rich tomato-vegetable broth. The large, white, fleshy beans are called "gigantes," which means gigantic—large lima beans are the closest thing you'll find here up to the task for this hearty recipe, which must be served with crusty whole grain bread to sop up the sauce at the bottom of the bowl.

SERVES 8

2 cups dried large lima beans

4 cups water

1 onion, diced

3 cloves garlic, minced

3 carrots, diced

½ cup tomato paste

1 teaspoon oregano

1 teaspoon rosemary

1 teaspoon marjoram

½ teaspoon thyme

¼ teaspoon black pepper

Salt to taste

1½ tablespoons extra-virgin olive oil

Place beans in a pot, cover with water, and soak overnight.

Drain water, add 4 cups fresh water, onion, garlic, carrots, tomato paste, oregano, rosemary, marjoram, thyme, and black pepper.

Cover, bring to a boil, reduce heat to medium-low, and simmer for about 1½ hours. Stir occasionally. Add water to replace that lost to condensation. Should make a thick, stew-like consistency.

Season with salt, as desired. Drizzle with olive oil. Serve immediately.

Nutrition information per serving: 204 calories, 3 g total fat, 1g saturated fat, 0 mg cholesterol, 40 mg sodium, 35 g carbohydrates, 10 g fiber, 8 g sugar, 11 g protein

Cold Cucumber Avocado Soup

Cold creamy soups are so refreshing, even on the warmest of days. The cool, verdant shades of avocados, cucumbers, green onions, cilantro, and lime shine in this herbal soup, which is as light and fresh as it is utterly delicious.

SERVES 8

2 large English cucumbers, with peel, quartered

2 avocados, ripe, peeled, pitted, quartered

2 green onions, chopped into thirds

2 garlic cloves

2 tablespoons fresh cilantro

¼ jalapeño pepper

¼ cup fresh lime or lemon juice

½ cup water

½ cup plant-based milk, plain, unsweetened

Pinch salt and pepper (optional)

Place all items in a large blender and process on low until very smooth.

Transfer to a covered container and chill well (about 2 hours) before serving.

Nutrition information per serving: 130 calories, 11 g total fat, 4 g saturated fat, 8 mg sodium, 4 g carbohydrates, 9 g fiber, 2 g sugar, 2 g protein

Syrian Orange Bulgur Salad

Key Mediterranean ingredients come together to create this simple salad, including bulgur, oranges, pine nuts, mint, and basil—tossed together with a fresh lemon and olive oil vinaigrette. It's a satisfying dish that serves as the main event, paired with a lentil soup, a potluck contribution, or a meal prep recipe to enjoy during the week.

SERVES 8

For the salad:

2 cups water

1 cup fine bulgur

2 medium oranges, peeled, chopped

1 cucumber, unpeeled, chopped

½ cup pine nuts

¼ cup fresh mint, chopped

¼ cup fresh basil, chopped

For the lemon olive oil vinaigrette:

1½ tablespoons extra-virgin olive oil

1 lemon, juiced

1 tablespoon pomegranate molasses (see *Note*)

1 clove garlic, minced

¼ teaspoon allspice

1 teaspoon cumin

¼ teaspoon cayenne pepper

Salt to taste (optional)

Place water in a medium pot, cover it, and bring to a boil. Turn off heat, add bulgur, stir quickly, cover, and let sit for 7 minutes. Remove lid and fluff with a fork. Allow bulgur to cool.

Mix cooled bulgur with oranges, cucumber, pine nuts, mint, and basil.

To make the lemon olive oil vinaigrette: In a small dish, whisk together olive oil, lemon juice, pomegranate molasses, garlic, allspice, cumin, cayenne pepper, and salt to taste (optional).

Pour dressing over salad and mix to distribute. Adjust seasonings as needed. Chill until serving time.

Note: Pomegranate molasses is a traditional Mediterranean ingredient based on reduced pomegranate juice. If you can't find it, substitute agave syrup in this recipe.

Nutrition information per serving: 179 calories, 9 g total fat, 1 g saturated fat, 0 mg cholesterol, 5 mg sodium, 24 g carbohydrates, 5 g fiber, 5 g sugar, 4 g protein

Overnight Oats with Spiced Figs and Dates

One of my favorite healthy, plant-based, on-the-go breakfasts is overnight oats. Make these in a single-serving mason jar the night before, then just add your toppings the next morning, and it's grab and go. You can enjoy these oats chilled, or heat them up for a comforting breakfast. You can even make up a few overnight oat containers all at once for multiple breakfasts during the week. This easy version of overnight oats celebrates the Mediterranean in all its glory, thanks to the decadence of ripe figs, the spicy sweetness of Chinese 5 spice, and the staying power of walnuts and chia seeds—plus a touch of blackstrap molasses. If figs are out of season, you can substitute dried figs.

SERVES 1

½ cup old-fashioned oats

¾ cup plant-based milk, plain, unsweetened

1 teaspoon blackstrap molasses

¼ teaspoon Chinese 5 spice seasoning blend

2 figs, sliced

¼ cup chopped walnuts

1 teaspoon chia seeds

Place oats in a mason jar or 2-cup container. Add plant-based milk, molasses, and spice blend and stir. Cover with lid and refrigerate overnight.

The next morning, add figs, walnuts, and chia seeds and enjoy!

Note: If you prefer your oats warm, heat the container in the microwave for 2 minutes before adding toppings.

Nutrition information per serving: 413 calories, 16 g total fat, 2 g saturated fat, 70 mg sodium, 58 g carbohydrates, 10 g fiber, 21 g sugar, 14 g protein

Fattoush Salad with Grilled Summer Vegetables

Fattoush salad—a crisp romaine lettuce salad filled with crunchy pieces of toasted pita bread—exemplifies the Mediterranean concept of making something of nothing. Why discard the leftover bread, when it can be turned into a salad the next day? In this version, I add the bounty of summer vegetables—eggplant, zucchini, peppers, tomatoes, onions—grilled to perfection before they are piled onto the salad bowl. Topped off with a dressing rich in the Middle Eastern spice sumac, it's pure healthy indulgence.

SERVES 8

For the vegetables:

1 small eggplant (such as Japanese), sliced horizontally

1 small summer squash (yellow or zucchini), sliced horizontally

1 small red bell pepper, sliced

1 cup cherry tomatoes (yellow or red)

1 small red onion, sliced

For the marinade/ dressing:

3 tablespoons extra-virgin olive oil

3 tablespoons fresh lemon juice

2 cloves garlic, minced

2 teaspoons thyme

2 teaspoons sumac

¼ teaspoon salt (optional)

¼ teaspoon black pepper

To prepare the vegetables: Prep vegetables, as directed, and place in a large dish.

To prepare the marinade: In a small dish mix together the olive oil, lemon juice, garlic, thyme, sumac, salt (optional), and pepper. Makes about ½ cup marinade.

Pour ¼ cup of the marinade over the vegetable mixture. Toss together with tongs to distribute. Allow to marinade for about 1 hour.

To grill the vegetables: Preheat grill to medium setting. Grill the vegetables until golden brown and just tender (about 8–12 minutes), turning and removing from grill when vegetables are done (a grill basket may come in handy so the vegetables don't fall through the cracks of the grill). Some vegetables will cook more quickly (onions, cherry tomatoes), while some may take longer (eggplant, squash, peppers).

To serve: While vegetables are grilling, drizzle 1 tablespoon of the marinade over the pita bread and place on the grill. Cook until golden and crunchy (about 5 minutes). Tear into bite-sized chunks.

In a large salad bowl, place romaine lettuce, fresh mint leaves, olives, and pieces of pita bread. Drizzle remaining marinade over salad and toss together.

Arrange grilled vegetables on top of salad and serve immediately.

For the pita bread:

2 whole grain pita bread

For the salad:

1 small head (about 4 cups)
romaine lettuce, chopped

½ cup chopped fresh mint
leaves

½ cup kalamata olives, pitted,
drained

Note: If you don't want to use the grill for this recipe, you can roast the vegetables and pita in the oven. Preheat the oven to 400°F. Arrange marinated vegetables on a baking sheet and place on the top rack; roast for about 40 minutes, until golden brown and tender. Place pita with marinade on a baking sheet in the oven at 400°F and bake for about 6 minutes, until slightly crisp and golden.

Nutrition information per serving: 155 calories, 8 g total fat, 1 g saturated fat, 0 mg cholesterol, 183 mg sodium, 21 g carbohydrates, 6 g fiber, 5 g sugar, 4 g protein

Dark Chocolate Pistachio Biscotti

I love the simple, earnest quality of biscotti, that twice-baked Italian treat that elevates everything from espresso to seasonal fruit to sorbet. This recipe for Dark Chocolate Pistachio Biscotti is moderate in sugar and even packed with whole grains. Make up a batch in advance to enjoy during the week, for lunch boxes, coffee breaks, and entertaining. I like to bake these up and store them in the freezer, then pull them out for treats. All you have to do is make the dough, shape into a log, bake the dough log, slice it into thin strips, and bake it again.

SERVES 32

2 tablespoons chia seeds

½ cup plant-based milk, plain, unsweetened

1 teaspoon vanilla

1 teaspoon apple cider vinegar

½ cup dairy-free margarine spread

¾ cup organic cane sugar

1 cup whole wheat flour

1¼ cups white flour

2 tablespoons cornstarch

¼ cup cocoa powder

1 teaspoon cinnamon

¼ teaspoon salt (optional)

½ cup dairy-free dark chocolate chips

½ cup pistachios, shelled

Mix chia seeds, plant-based milk, vanilla, and apple cider vinegar in a bowl and let stand for 10 minutes.

Preheat oven to 350°F.

Mix margarine and sugar in an electric mixer until creamy. Add chia seeds mixture and mix until smooth.

Stir together flours, cornstarch, cocoa powder, cinnamon, and salt (optional) and mix well. Gradually add dry ingredients to electric mixer bowl and mix until smooth. Should make a stiff dough.

Stir in chocolate chips and pistachios by hand.

Remove dough from bowl and divide into two equal parts. On parchment paper, roll out each piece of dough to approximately 4 inches wide by 11 inches long by 1 inch thick.

Place the parchment paper with dough on baking sheets and bake for 20 minutes.

Reduce temperature to 300°F. Remove dough from oven and allow to cool slightly. Slice into ½-inch-thick strips and place on parchment paper lined baking sheets with cut side up.

Bake at 300°F for about 8 minutes, then turn over to other side and bake for about 8 minutes, until slightly dry and golden brown.

Remove from oven, cool, and store in airtight containers.

Nutrition information per serving: 107 calories, 5 g total fat, 2 g saturated fat, 3 mg cholesterol, 22 mg sodium, 14 g carbohydrates, 2 g fiber, 6 g sugar, 2 g protein

Farro Bowl with Pomegranates and Cucumbers

Pomegranates offer a cheerful ruby touch to the cooler days, when other produce wanes. Grown both in the Mediterranean and California's Central Coast, these sweet/tart seeds offer so much flavor and dimension to a variety of dishes. The glistening beauty of pomegranate seeds against a canvas of crunchy whole grain farro, with sliced herbal cucumbers and juicy mandarins with a creamy plant-based yogurt dressing, comes together to create one of my favorite recipes.

SERVES 4

For the farro:

1½ cups farro, uncooked

4½ cups water

Pinch salt

For the pomegranate cucumber salad:

½ cup pomegranate arils (seeds)

3 Persian cucumbers, sliced

2 mandarin oranges, peeled, separated into segments

4 green onions, sliced

½ cup coarsely chopped fresh mint leaves

2 cloves garlic, minced

1½ tablespoons extra-virgin olive oil

1 tablespoon lemon juice

½ teaspoon ground coriander

¼ teaspoon black pepper

For the vegan yogurt dressing:

1 5-ounce container cultured plant-based yogurt, plain, unsweetened (soy, almond, cashew)

1 clove garlic, minced

1 tablespoon lemon juice

½ teaspoon thyme

½ teaspoon cumin

Pinch sea salt and ground black pepper

For the garnish:

½ teaspoon sumac

4 teaspoons sesame seeds

To prepare the farro: Cook farro in a medium pot with water and salt. Simmer over medium heat for about 25–30 minutes, until grains are just starting to crack open. Drain off any remaining water, and cool until it is at room temperature.

To prepare the pomegranate cucumber salad: In a medium mixing bowl, combine pomegranates, cucumbers, orange segments, green onions, mint, garlic, olive oil, lemon juice, coriander, and black pepper together.

To prepare the vegan yogurt dressing: In a small bowl, mix together plant-based yogurt with garlic, lemon juice, thyme, cumin, and salt and pepper until smooth.

To assemble the bowls (makes four): Fill each individual bowl (about 2 cups serving size) with:

One-fourth (about ¾ cup) of the cooked, cooled farro in the base of the bowl.

Top with one-fourth (about 1 cup) of the pomegranate cucumber salad.

Dot with one-fourth (about 3 tablespoons) of the yogurt dressing.

Sprinkle with a pinch sumac and 1 teaspoon sesame seeds over each bowl.

Serve immediately.

Nutrition information per serving: 418 calories, 10 g total fat, 1 g saturated fat, 0 mg cholesterol, 29 mg sodium, 69 g carbohydrates, 8 g fiber, 13 g sugar, 14 g protein

Rustic Nectarine Panzanella Salad

Italian cuisine also has a bread-saving tradition, making sure to find everyday uses for leftover, stale bread. The classic peasant food, panzanella salad, is filled with torn, crisp bread, tomatoes, and cucumbers—of course with a generous splash of olive oil and vinegar. But why stop there? I used this basic food tradition to create a gorgeous summer salad bursting with beautiful, ripe nectarines, heirloom tomatoes, and cucumbers.

SERVES 8

For the bread:

Half of 1.2-pound loaf of rustic, whole grain bread

1 tablespoon extra-virgin olive oil

Freshly ground black pepper (as desired)

For the salad:

2 firm yet ripe nectarines, unpeeled, thinly sliced

2 large heirloom tomatoes, sliced into thin wedges

3 green onions, sliced

2 small cucumbers, unpeeled, sliced

½ cup fresh basil leaves, chopped

For the red wine vinaigrette:

1½ tablespoons extra-virgin olive oil

2 tablespoons red wine vinegar

1 teaspoon Dijon mustard

1 small clove garlic, minced

Salt and pepper (as desired)

Preheat oven to 400°F.

To prepare the bread: Tear whole grain bread into bite-sized chunks (about 1-inch) and place in a baking dish. Drizzle with 1 tablespoon olive oil, sprinkle with freshly ground black pepper (as desired), and place on top rack of oven. Bake for about 10–12 minutes, until barely crisp and golden brown on surface (do not overcook). Remove from oven and set aside to cool.

To prepare the salad: Toss together nectarines, tomatoes, onions, cucumbers, and basil leaves in a mixing bowl. Toss in cooled, toasted bread pieces.

To prepare the red wine vinaigrette: In a small dish, whisk together 1½ tablespoons olive oil, vinegar, mustard, garlic, and salt and pepper (as desired).

Toss vinaigrette into the salad ingredients.

Serve immediately.

Nutrition information per serving: 156 calories, 6 g total fat, 1 g saturated fat, 143 mg sodium, 0 mg cholesterol, 22 g carbohydrates, 4 g fiber, 7 g sugar, 6 g protein

16

Wrapping It All Up

Now it's time to embrace the true California plant-powered spirit and simply dive in! In these chapters, I've hopefully given you stories to inspire your lifestyle, and ideas to enliven your culinary habits. Even if you don't live in California, I believe that each and every one of these recipes can be made in your own home kitchen, based on ingredients and foods that you will find and cherish. I hope that you will dig up a small piece of earth, whether in your garden or a pot on your balcony, to grow a plant or two in the warm, long days of summer. I trust that you will get to know local food growers in your neighborhood and join in on the beauty of the best and most bountiful of plant foods, which can nurture and heal your mind, body, and soul. I believe that you will get in touch with your cultural roots and try to dig out plant-based traditions dear to those who came before you.

A harvest of blood oranges from my backyard garden highlights the abundance of citrus fruits available in this sun-drenched state.

Here are a few more tips for eating a bountiful plant-based diet, along with a cache of tried-and-true recipes for your sunny new outlook on life.

Eat Like a Californian

From east to west, north to south, these are some of my favorite eating tips that can let the sunshine into your plant-based lifestyle.

- Don't be afraid of eating veggies for breakfast. Hey, avocados on your breakfast sandwich, sprouts on your breakfast wrap, snow peas on your tahini toast. It's not that hard to do, and the flavor and health potential will skyrocket.

- Run to global food, as fast as you can. Don't ever shy away from a food culture or global eatery you never met. Plant-based eating experiences await you! From banana flower salad (Thailand) to vegan goulash (Hungarian), a world of eating discovery lies just around the corner.

- It's ok to be a bit glam. You do eat with your eyes, after all. And plants are what offer true beauty and color to the plate—just ask any chef. From the perfect pearl of a new spring pea to the pop of pink in Easter egg radishes to violets at the side of your plate, plants are true masterpieces. Dutch masters knew all about the sheer beauty of edible plants, as they reveled in a ripe, split fig or pomegranate and reflective cluster of grapes on the canvas centuries ago. So, follow suit and make your food something to gawk at.

- Open your eyes to a more biodiverse diet. Plant-based eating is so much more than tofu, frozen hockey puck veggie burgers, and brown rice (though these are all fine and good). Discover new and intriguing vegetables, such as spiky purple kohlrabi, white speckled dragon fruit, and neon orange-red kuri squash. You can eat like this every day!

- Think of cooking as meditation. I know, you get home at the end of a busy day, and the last thing you want to do is figure out how to fill your growling belly. So, you do what everyone does: order takeout. But, you know, in some cultures, cooking is considered a reverent act. To have the good fortune and ability to walk into a well-stocked kitchen, assemble healthful foods, and prepare them in a delicious way that will nourish and enrich the lives of your loved ones is a thing to approach with gratitude. As the onions are simmering and the spices are toasting, take a deep breath, let the day's burdens fall off your shoulders, and enjoy the sights, smells, sounds, and tastes of cooking plant-based foods.

- Save the planet. Yes, you can make a difference with your fork. You can lighten your steps on Mother Earth by eating a vegan diet based on sustainably produced whole plant foods. After all, research shows that your plant-based eating style has the lowest environmental footprint compared to other diet patterns. So, go about your day, knowing you are doing your best to lower greenhouse gas emissions and the amount of water and land needed to produce food by eating the way you do.

- Save the animals. The other thing you can feel good about today is that you are not only eating a diet that reduces the amount of land required to grow food, thus preserving natural habitat for countless species, but that you are also lessening the burden of animals suffering due to animal agriculture—simply by the way you eat.

- Smile, you've got this! And finally, don't forget to absorb some of that good old sunny spirit and have fun with your plant-based eating style. It is not a cross to bear. Eating plant-based is a joy—a revelation! Let this book serve as testimony to the beauty and light surrounding a California vegan lifestyle.

Cranberry Oat Pilaf

Plant-based eating should effortlessly wind its way through the seasons of your life, including holidays. This is one of my favorite one-dish easy recipes to serve at my holiday table. With only a skillet and a few key ingredients—celery, garlic, mushrooms, cranberries, pistachios, and oats—you can create a gorgeous, flavorful side dish to go with anything.

SERVES 8

1 teaspoon extra-virgin olive oil

1 small onion, diced

3 stalks celery with leaves, diced

1 clove garlic, minced

½ cup chopped mushrooms

2 tablespoons chopped fresh parsley

¼ teaspoon turmeric

1 teaspoon marjoram

½ teaspoon black pepper

⅓ cup pistachios

1 cup fresh whole cranberries (or canned or frozen)

1 tablespoon pure maple syrup

2 cups vegetable broth

1½ cups old-fashioned oats, gluten-free

Heat oil in a large cast iron skillet. Add onions, celery, and garlic and sauté for 5 minutes.

Add mushrooms, parsley, turmeric, marjoram, black pepper, and pistachios and sauté for an additional 3 minutes.

While vegetables are cooking, heat oven to 350°F.

Add cranberries, maple syrup, broth, and oats, stirring until smooth.

Transfer skillet to oven and bake on top rack for 25 minutes, until golden and tender.

Nutrition information per serving: 160 calories, 5 g total fat, 1 g saturated fat, 160 mg sodium, 26 g carbohydrates, 5 g fiber, 2 g sugar, 8 g protein

Blueberry Millet Muffins

These scrumptious vegan muffins are filled with whole grain goodness—even millet, which offers a crunchy, yet fluffy bite. Use fresh berries when they're in season, or dried berries when they're not. You can whip them up in minutes with many ingredients you already have in your kitchen. The chia and flaxseeds offer a great alternative to eggs in this recipe, and provide a boost of healthy omega-3 fatty acids too.

SERVES 6

¾ cup plant-based milk, plain, unsweetened

1 teaspoon vanilla

1 tablespoon chia seeds

1 tablespoon flaxseeds, ground

⅓ cup vegetable oil

½ cup white whole wheat flour

½ cup millet flour

½ cup all-purpose wheat flour

2 teaspoons baking powder

Pinch salt

⅓ cup coconut palm sugar (or brown sugar)

½ cup dried blueberries (or small fresh)

Preheat oven to 375°F.

Whip together plant-based milk, vanilla, chia, flax, and oil for 2 minutes to create a thick mixture.

Stir in flours, baking powder, salt, and coconut palm sugar only until moistened.

Stir in blueberries.

Spray a muffin pan with nonstick spray (or use muffin liners).

Fill muffin cups with ⅓ cup batter.

Bake for about 30 minutes, until tender and golden.

Remove from oven and let rest for 5 minutes. Remove from muffin pan and serve immediately.

Nutrition information per muffin: 284 calories, 14 g total fat, 1 g saturated fat, 0 mg cholesterol, 22 mg sodium, 38 g carbohydrates, 5 g fiber, 14 g sugar, 5 g protein

Chickpea Shakshuka

Take a hot, trendy recipe and make it 100% plant-based. That's my mantra. Enter shakshuka, the North African dish that features eggs in a spicy tomato sauce. Shakshuka is on everyone's radar these days, and it can easily be made vegan—no fuss indeed—by swapping out eggs for chickpeas.

SERVES 6

1 tablespoon extra-virgin olive oil

1 medium onion, chopped

3 cloves garlic, minced

1 red bell pepper, chopped

2 teaspoons smoked paprika

1 teaspoon fennel seeds

1 teaspoon cumin seeds

¼ teaspoon cinnamon

¼ teaspoon cayenne pepper

1 tablespoon brown sugar

1 28-ounce can diced tomatoes, with liquid

1 15-ounce can chickpeas, drained

¼ cup chopped fresh cilantro

1 small loaf (about 12 ounces) rustic whole grain bread, sliced into 1-inch pieces

Heat olive oil in a large skillet.

Add onions, garlic, and bell pepper and sauté for 5 minutes.

Add smoked paprika, fennel seeds, cumin seeds, cinnamon, cayenne pepper, and brown sugar and sauté for 1 minute.

Add diced tomatoes and chickpeas, cover, and simmer over medium heat for 10 minutes, stirring occasionally.

Remove lid and allow to simmer for an additional 5 minutes, until thick and bubbly.

While shakshuka is simmering, place slices of whole grain bread in a toaster, toaster oven, or oven and toast until crisp and golden brown.

Dish up shakshuka into individual bowls and serve with toasted bread.

Makes about 1 cup shakshuka with two slices bread per serving.

Nutrition information per serving: 300 calories, 6 g total fat, 1 g saturated fat, 462 mg sodium, 0 mg cholesterol, 52 g carbohydrates, 9 g fiber, 12 g sugar, 13 g protein

Peanut Berry Scones

These healthy, nutrient-rich scones are packed with plant foods, and low in sugar and oil. In fact, my Peanut Berry Scones are pure vegan bliss! They make great healthy treats for kids and adults alike. Plus, they are so aromatic, flavorful, and downright pretty. Not to mention easy! Just mix up the dough in minutes, roll it out, slice it into wedges, and pop them in the oven. I love to use peanut flour—rich in flavor and nutrition—in baked goods, such as these scones. You can find it in most natural food stores, or online.

SERVES 8

2 cups white whole wheat flour (may use half whole wheat + half all-purpose flour, if desired)

¾ cup peanut flour

1 tablespoon baking powder

Pinch salt (optional)

¼ cup sugar

¼ cup vegetable oil

1 cup plant-based milk, plain, unsweetened

¼ cup dried wild blueberries

Preheat oven to 375°F.

Mix together flours, baking powder, salt (optional), and sugar.

Stir in oil and plant-based milk just until well combined. Should make a slightly sticky, soft dough.

Stir in blueberries.

Flour a cutting board surface and roll out dough to make a thick circle, about 10 inches in diameter.

Cut circle into eight pie-shaped wedges.

Spray a baking sheet with nonstick cooking spray and arrange scones on sheet.

Bake for about 20 minutes, until golden brown and cooked through.

Serve warm.

Nutrition information per serving: 144 calories, 5 g total fat, 0 g saturated fat, 17 mg sodium, 0 mg cholesterol, 23 g carbohydrates, 3 g fiber, 8 g sugar, 3 g protein

Balsamic Eggplant Tofu Stacks with Quinoa

I love the art of layering vegetables into pretty little stacks, and then anointing them with a flavorful sauce. It's a special way to make plant-based eating elegant. This recipe features a bed of quinoa, with a stack of eggplant, onions, portobello mushrooms, tofu, and tomatoes perched atop, and a rich marinara sauce cascading over it all.

SERVES 6

For the quinoa:

1 cup tri-color quinoa, uncooked

2 cups vegetable broth

For the eggplant tofu stacks:

1 medium eggplant (about 2½–3 inches in diameter)

1 medium onion

1 15-ounce package extra firm tofu, drained

1 large portobello mushroom

1½ tablespoons extra-virgin olive oil

1½ tablespoons balsamic vinegar

1 clove garlic, minced

Pinch each of black pepper and sea salt

2 medium tomatoes (about 3 inches in diameter), sliced about ¼ inch thick

For the topping:

1¼ cups marinara sauce

½ teaspoon Italian seasoning blend

To prepare the quinoa: Place quinoa in a small pot and add vegetable broth. Cover and cook, stirring occasionally, until just tender—about 12 minutes. Remove from heat and fluff with a fork.

While grains are cooking, preheat oven to 375°F to make eggplant tofu stacks.

To prepare the eggplant tofu stacks: Slice eggplant into twelve about ¼-inch-thick slices.

Slice onion into six about ¼-inch-thick slices.

Slice tofu horizontally into three sections (about ¼ inch thick). Use a round cookie or biscuit cutter (or a drinking glass) to cut into six circles about 2½–3 inches in diameter.

Save remaining tofu for another recipe, such as Scrambled Turmeric Tofu).

Slice portobello mushrooms into six thin vertical slices.

Arrange vegetables and tofu on a large baking sheet.

Mix olive oil, balsamic vinegar, garlic, black pepper, and sea salt in a small dish.

Drizzle over vegetables and tofu.

Place baking sheet in oven on top shelf and roast for about 30 minutes, until vegetables are tender and browned.

While vegetables are roasting, heat marinara sauce and Italian seasoning blend until warm.

To serve: Mound cooked quinoa on individual dinner plates (about ½ cup per plate) or the entire batch on a large family-style platter. Prepare six vegetable tofu stacks as follows: one slice eggplant, one slice tofu, one slice fresh tomato, one slice mushrooms, and one slice eggplant. Spoon 3 tablespoons marinara sauce over each stack and dust with a pinch of Italian seasoning.

Serve immediately.

Nutrition information per serving: 270 calories, 8 g total fat, 1 g saturated fat, 458 mg sodium, 0 mg cholesterol, 39 g carbohydrates, 8 g fiber, 12 g sugar, 12 g protein

Sheet Pan Winter Vegetables with Za'atar

One of my favorite ways to get a really healthy, delicious, versatile meal on the table in minutes is with my trusty sheet pan, which I've had for over thirty years now! All I do is chop up whatever veggies I have on hand, drizzle on a flavorful vinaigrette, and pop it in the oven to roast to golden perfection. Then all you have to do is pair it with a plant protein and you're all set. If you've not tried this go-to meal preparation, this recipe—featuring winter vegetables and North African seasonings—will convince you of how it needs to be part of your regular culinary repertoire.

SERVES 8

For the vegetables:

2 cups sliced red or white cabbage

1 small (1 pound) acorn squash, peeled, cubed

3 beets, trimmed

2 medium Yukon gold potatoes, unpeeled, cubed

1 red onion, sliced

For the vinaigrette:

2 tablespoons extra-virgin olive oil

1 tablespoon pomegranate molasses (see *Note*)

1 tablespoon lemon juice

3 cloves garlic, minced

¼ teaspoon salt

½ teaspoon black pepper

For the topping:

¼ cup chopped fresh parsley

1 tablespoon za'atar

Preheat oven to 400°F.

On a baking sheet, arrange vertical rows of cabbage, squash, beets, potatoes, and red onion.

In a small dish, mix together olive oil, pomegranate molasses, lemon juice, garlic, salt, and black pepper.

Drizzle the vinaigrette evenly over the vegetables. With tongs, distribute vinaigrette into vegetables in each row.

Place on top rack of oven and roast until tender and golden (40–45 minutes).

Remove from oven, sprinkle with fresh parsley and za'atar, and serve.

Note: Pomegranate molasses is a traditional Mediterranean ingredient based on reduced pomegranate juice. If you can't find it, substitute agave syrup in this recipe.

Nutrition information per serving: 121 calories, 4 g total fat, 1 g saturated fat, 0 mg cholesterol, 108 mg sodium, 22 g carbohydrates, 4 g fiber, 5 g sugar, 2 g protein

Lentilicious Mango Turmeric Smoothie

You'll never guess that the plant power behind this smoothie is the humble lentil. It's packed with protein, fiber, and antioxidants to help you start your day right.

SERVES 2

1 cup cooked lentils (brown, yellow, or red), chilled

2 cups chopped fresh (chilled) or frozen mangos

½ cup plant-based milk, unsweetened, plain, chilled

½ cup orange juice, chilled

1-inch fresh turmeric root

Place lentils, mangos, plant-based milk, orange juice, and fresh turmeric root in a blender.

Process until smooth and creamy.

Pour into two large glasses and enjoy.

Makes about 1½ cups per serving.

Nutrition information per serving: 282 calories, 2 g total fat, 0 g saturated fat, 0 mg cholesterol, 28 mg sodium, 58 g carbohydrates, 12 g fiber, 32 g sugar, 12 g protein

References

Anderson, M. K. (2013). *Tending the Wild*. Oakland, California: University of California Press. This book details the history of Native Americans in California, and offers an overview of native land management that includes ecological practices.

Behrens, P., Kiefte-de Jong, J. C., Bosker, T., Rodrigues, F. D., de Koning, A., & Tukker, A. (2017, December 4). Evaluating the environmental impacts of dietary recommendations. *PNAS*. Retrieved from: http://www.pnas.org/content/early/2017/11/28/1711889114.

Blitz, M. (2016, August 22). The History of Vegetarianism: From Plant-Eating Neanderthals to "Diet for a Small Planet." Retrieved from: https://www.foodandwine.com/news/history-vegetarianism.

Bordelon, M. (2012, March). Geologic Overview of Southern California Mountain Ranges. Retrieved from: https://olliuci.files.wordpress.com/2012/03/uci-talk-geology-of-socal-mountains-3-19-12.pdf.

Brittanica. (n.d.) 8 of History's Most Famus Vegetarians. Retrieved from: https://www.britannica.com/list/8-of-historys-most-famous-vegetarians.

Buettner, D. (2012). *The Blue Zones: 9 Lessons for Living Longer from the People Who've Lived the Longest*. Washington, D.C.: National Geographic.

California Department of Food and Agriculture. (2016). California Agricultural Statistics Review 2015-2016. Retrieved from: https://www.cdfa.ca.gov/statistics/PDFs/2016Report.pdf.

California Department of Food and Agriculture. Certified Farmers Market Program. Retrieved from: https://www.cdfa.ca.gov/is/i_&_c/cfm.html.

California Department of Food and Agriculture & State Board of Food and Agriculture. (2010, December). California Agricultural Vision: Strategies for Sustainability. Retrieved from: https://www.cdfa.ca.gov/agvision/docs/Ag_Vision_Final_Report_Dec_2010.pdf.

Dutschke, D. (2014, October 8). A History of American Indians in California. Retrieved from: http://ohp.parks.ca.gov/pages/1054/files/american%20indians%20in%20california.pdf.

FAO. (2009). The State of Food and Agriculture. Retrieved from: http://www.fao.org/docrep/012/i0680e/i0680e.pdf.

Fehrenbacher, D. E. (1964). *A Basic History of California*. Princeton, NJ: Van Nostrand.

Fry, P. L., DePuydt, R. E., & Walker, C. (2017). *The Ojai Valley: An Illustrated History*. Ojai, CA: Ojai Valley Museum.

Hallstrom, E., Gee, Q., Scarborough, P., & Cleveland, D. A. (2107, March 6). A healthier US diet could reduce greenhouse gas emissions from both the food and health care systems. *Climactic Change*. 142: 199-212. Retrieved from: https://link.springer.com/article/10.1007%2Fs10584-017-1912-5.

Heizer, R. F., & Whipple, M. A. (1971). *The California Indians: A Source Book*. University of California Press, 1971 Second Edition.

IFIC. (2017). Food & Health Survey. Retrieved from: http://www.foodinsight.org/sites/default/files/2017-ExSum-FoodValues_0.pdf.

Jackson, R. H., & Gardzina, A. Agriculture, Drought, and Chumash Congregation in California Missions (1782-1834). California Missions Foundation. Retrieved from: http://californiamissionsfoundation.org/articles/agriculturedroughtandchumashcongregation.

Jones, A. D., Hoey, L., Blesh, J., Miller, L., Green, A., & Shapiro, L. F. (2016, July 11). A Systematic Review of the Measurement of Sustainable Diets. *Advances in Nutrition* 4: 641-664. Retrieved from: https://academic.oup.com/advances/article/7/4/641/4568677.

Kahleova, H., Levin, S., & Barnard, N. (2017, August 9). Cardio-Metabolic Benefits of Plant-Based Diets. *Nutrients.* 9:8. Retrieved from: https://www.ncbi.nlm.nih.gov/pmc/articles/PMC5579641/.

Klonsky, K. (2010). A Look at California's Organic Agriculture Production. *ARE Update,* 14, 8-11. Retrieved from: https://www.cdfa.ca.gov/is/pdfs/A_Look_at_California%27s_Organic_Agriculture_Production.pdf.

Lappé, F. M. (1971). *Diet for a Small Planet.* New York, NY: Ballantine Books.

Loma Linda University School of Public Health. (n.d.). History of the Adventist Health Studies. Retrieved from: https://publichealth.llu.edu/adventist-health-studies/about/history-adventist-health-studies.

Meier, T., & Christen, O. (2013, January 15). Environmental impacts of dietary recommendations and dietary styles. *Environ Sci Technol.* 47:877-88. Retrieved from: https://pubs.acs.org/doi/full/10.1021/es302152v.

Melina, V., Craig, W., & Levin, S. (2016, December). Position of the Academy of Nutrition and Dietetics: Vegetarian Diets. *J Acad Nutr Diet.* 12: 1970-1980. Retrieved from: https://www.eatrightpro.org/~/media/eatrightpro files/practice/position and practice papers/position papers/vegetarian-diet.ashx.

Miller, C. I. Geologic, Climatic, and Vegetation History of California. US Forest Service. Retrieved from: https://www.fs.fed.us/psw/publications/millar/psw_2012_millar003.pdf.

Mintel. (2016, July 11). Vegan food and drink product launches outpace vegetarian. Retrieved from: http://www.mintel.com/press-centre/food-and-drink/vegan-food-and-drink-product-launches-outpace-vegetarian-in-germany.

Mullen, N. (2003). California Indian Food and Culture. Retrieved from: http://www.tongvapeople.org/wp-content/uploads/2016/05/Hearst-Museum-teaching-kit.pdf.

Nuccitelli, D. (2018, September 17). California plans to show the world how to meet the Paris climate target. *The Guardian.* Retrieved from: https://www.theguardian.com/environment/climate-consensus-97-per-cent/2018/sep/17/california-plans-to-show-the-world-how-to-meet-the-paris-climate-target

Oldways. (n.d.). African Heritage Diet. Retrieved from: https://oldwayspt.org/traditional-diets/african-heritage-diet

Pan, A., Sun, Q., Bernstein, A. M., Schulze, M. B., Manson, J. E., Stampfer, M. J.,...Hu, F. B. (2012, March 12). Red Meat Consumption and Mortality. *Archives of Internal Medicine.* 7: 555-563. Retrieved from: https://www.ncbi.nlm.nih.gov/pmc/articles/PMC3712342/.

Rosi, A., Mena, P., Pellegrini, N., Turroni, S. Neviani, E. Ferrocino, I.,...Scazzina, F. (2017, June 2). Environmental impact of omnivorous, ovo-lacto-vegetarian, and vegan diet. *Nature.* Retrieved from: https://www.nature.com/articles/s41598-017-06466-8.

Rowland, M. P. (2018, March 23). Mellenials Are Driving the Worldwide Shift Away from Meat. Forbes. Retrieved from: https://www.forbes.com/sites/michael pellmanrowland/2018/03/23/millennials-move-away-from-meat/#7b31a9dba4a4.

Sabate, J., & Soret, S. (2014, June 4). Sustainability of plant-based diets: back to the future. *Am J Clin Nutr.* 100:476S-482S. Retrieved from: http://ajcn.nutrition.org/content/100/Supplement_1/476S.full.

Siebert, J. (2003). California Agriculture Dimensions and Issues. University of California Giannini Foundation of Agricultural Economics, Division of Agriculture and Natural Resources. Retrieved from: https://s.giannini.ucop.edu/uploads/giannini_public/4e/a8/4ea8b9cc-df88-4146-b1ae-e5467736e104/escholarship_uc_item_9145n8m1.pdf.

Sustainable Conservation. California Agriculture and Climate Change Challenges and Opportunities for Profitability. Retrieved from: http://suscon.org/pdfs/cowpower/pdfs/CaliforniaAgricultureandClimateChange.pdf.

Tai Le, L., & Sabate, J. (2014, June). Beyond Meatless, the Health Effects of Vegan Diets: Findings from the Adventist Cohorts. *Nutrients.* 6: 2131-2147. Retrieved from: https://www.ncbi.nlm.nih.gov/pmc/articles/PMC4073139/.

Thompson, P. B. (2015). *From Field to Fork: Food Ethics for Everyone.* New York, NY: Oxford University Press.

The Vegetarian Resource Group. (2016). How Many Adults in the US Are Vegetarian or Vegan? Retrieved from: http://www.vrg.org/nutshell/Polls/2016_adults_veg.htm.

The Vegetarian Resource Group. (2016). Why do People Eat Vegetarian or Vegan Meals When Eating Out? Retrieved from: http://www.vrg.org/nutshell/Polls/2016_eating_out.htm.

Welch, R. (2006, July). Brief History of the Tongva Tribe. Retrieved from: http://tongvapeople.com/native_american_history.pdf.

Willett, W., Rockstrom, J., Loken, B., Springmann, M., Lang, T., Vermeulen, S., Garnett, T. (2019, January 16). Food in the Anthropocene: the EAT-Lancet Commission on healthy diets from sustainable food systems. *The Lancet.* Retrieved from: https://www.thelancet.com/journals/lancet/article/PIIS0140-6736(18)31788-4/fulltext?utm_campaign=tleat19&utm_source=hub_page.

Recipe Index

About the Author

Known as *The Plant-Powered Dietitian*, Sharon Palmer (MSFS, RDN) has established an award-winning career in the field of nutrition and sustainability. One of the most widely recognized registered dietitians in the world, Sharon is an accomplished writer, editor, blogger, author, speaker, and media expert. In particular, she has gained recognition for her expertise in plant-based nutrition and sustainability. Sharon has authored over 1,000 articles in a variety of publications, including *Better Homes and Gardens*, *Oprah Magazine*, and *LA Times*. Her previous books include *The Plant-Powered Diet: The Lifelong Eating Plan for Achieving Optimal Health, Beginning Today* and *Plant-Powered for Life: Eat Your Way to Lasting Health with 52 Simple Steps & 125 Delicious Recipes*. Sharon also has contributed to several book chapters on nutrition and sustainability. She serves as the nutrition editor for *Today's Dietitian*, associate faculty in the MS of Sustainable Food Systems Program at Prescott College, judge for the James Beard Journalism Awards, nutrition consultant for several organizations such as AICR and Oldways, and co-founder of Food and Planet. Sharon presents frequently at conferences, and is also a weekly contributing nutrition expert in the media, including print, online, radio, podcasts, television, social media, videos, and film. Sharon enjoys organizing farm and sustainability tours across the world, including her collaboration with Sterling College's Italian Alps annual tour. She recently completed her Master of Science in Sustainable Food Systems from Green Mountain College in Vermont. And she still has time to blog every day for her popular online community (400,000 members strong and growing) at *The Plant-Powered Dietitian*. Living in the sustainability mecca of Ojai, California, with her husband and two dogs, Sharon enjoys tending her own organic garden, visiting the local farmers market, volunteering in local environmental organizations, and cooking for friends and family.